did prince madog
discover america?

did prince madog
discover america?

an investigation by

michael senior

ISBN: 0-86381-899-4

*Published by
Gwasg Carreg Gwalch,
12 Iard yr Orsaf, Llanrwst, Wales, LL26 0EH.*
☎ *01492 642031* 🗎 *01492 641502*
*e-mail: books@carreg-gwalch.co.uk
website: www.carreg-gwalch.co.uk*

Printed and published in Wales.

PRINCE MADOC SAILED FROM HERE
ABER KERRIK GWYNAN 1170 A.D.
AND LANDED AT MOBILE ALABAMA
    WITH HIS SHIPS
GORN GWYNANT AND PEDR SANT

                    PLAQUE IN THE GARDEN OF
                    ODSTONE, RHOS ON SEA

contents

preface

There are not many things one can say with absolute certainty about Prince Madog ab Owain Gwynedd, but one, I think, is beyond dispute. Whoever he was – if indeed anyone – and whatever it was he did, he could not have imagined that, some 830 years later, he would give rise to references in about 182 sites on the Internet. So many books, theses, pamphlets and papers have, by now, been devoted to him, that it might seem foolhardy, not to say otiose, for me to add to them now. The fact is, however, that in all this disparate literature there is remarkably little agreement. Clearly there remains something to be got to the bottom of, a challenge which I am constantly loathe to refuse.

It is too much to hope, perhaps, that we can ever be certain of the truth, about Madog. The real question is: what has caused this situation in the first place, how did it come about that people have argued for so long that he did, or that he didn't, discover America.

His name and his exploit have, it turns out, been put to surprisingly varied uses. He has been used, for instance, twice, as British propaganda in international politics. He has been summoned as a witness in the cause of Welsh self-identity. In Welsh heroic literature he has been cited as an exemplar. Since the 16th century he has been coerced into drafting the historical world-map. Books and essays have been written, at least since the 19th century, debunking the whole project, just as, at the same time and with equal scholarship and with equal certainty, books and papers have been written proving its truth. Clearly this is too much of a burden to be borne by someone who simply didn't exist. There is at least the certainty that for a long time Madog has existed as a powerful idea, and indeed that he still does. Where did that come from, we may well ask, if not from the deeds of a 12th century Welsh prince?

Only a few writers on the subject have had the courage to say that in the end we do not know. There are hints and clues in profusion – which will be considered here – that a factual basis underlies the potent legend. There are areas of tantalising doubt, however, and we shall have to confront them. Yet still the ultimate question remains, and I shall try to answer it. Whether or not Madog did actually sail to America and set up a colony there; whether or not anyone has actually encountered his descendants: how did it happen that so many apparently sane and sober people have convinced themselves that these various things took place, and written them into traditional historical fact?

This book will inevitably be largely a round-up of the main works (and some minor ones) in the vast bulk of the Madog literature. It will also bring the matter up to date, recording the latest attested facts. It is, after all, some twenty-five years now since anyone has written a major book about Madog, and in some respects academic thinking on the related matters has changed since then. That is quite a long gap in Madogology, and perhaps the subject is due now for one of its periodic revivals.

the story

A long time ago, probably more than 10,000 years, the river Conwy flowed out to the sea near Penrhyn Bay, running down what is now the Dolwyd-Mochdre corridor, across the flat area now occupied by the Rhos-on-Sea (Llandrillo-yn-Rhos) golf course, which area was perhaps its delta. This outflow eventually got blocked by sea ice, ice sheets breaking off from the glaciers of Scotland to float unhindered down the Irish Sea until encountering our northern coast. The Conwy then banked up to form an enormous lake, before eventually breaking through the narrow rock ridge between the Vardre at Deganwy and the lower outcrops of Conwy Mountain, from then on to form its present estuary.

For a long time thereafter another river ran the course of the Conwy's former route. Known (as perhaps the original Conwy once was itself) as the Afon Ganol, the 'middle river' – middle, we may wonder, between what? – this meandered through its marshland until recent times, when most of it has been straightened, conduited and controlled. Now thus governed in conduit and culvert it takes the form for most of its course of a long straight ditch.

For most of its history in fact the Afon Ganol would be better viewed as a tidal feature, a strait, rather than a river, as it flowed (and indeed still flows) both ways at once, emptying the tributaries which fall into the Mochdre valley out into the Conwy near Glan Conwy Corner and out into the sea at Rhos. Sluice gates now prevent it from carrying back into the valley the waters of the flood-tides, and the massive breakwater at Penrhyn Bay and Rhos-on-Sea secures the golf club from disappearing under ten foot of water; but for centuries of recorded time it presented a swampy impediment to travel.

For a long time the mouth of this river formed a navigable inlet. A court case of 1687 (cited by the Reverend Venables Williams in his booklet *The Archaeological History of Llandrillo-yn-Rhos*) mentions ships of "20 or 30 tun" which "might at a certain time of flowing water gett in there". A certain Mr. Pugh built a bridge to connect two areas of swamp which he farmed and thus stopped "all boates and small vessels from getting in there for shelter in stormy weather."

The old course of the Ganol ran through what are now the gardens of a house called Odstone, the nearest to the golf club, from where, in 1965, the owner wrote to Richard Deacon (then researching his book *Madoc and the Discovery of America*) that she had lived there for 50 years "and my father always told me that Prince Madoc set sail for America and left from an old stone pier which is part of my garden…" The local historian Norman Tucker confirmed that there was a local tale to this effect, though he did not know the origin of it. Some thirty yards of the ancient quay still forms Odstone's rockery, the drive to the house passing over the top of it.

The earliest trace of Madog at this spot appears to have occurred in a work by Cynric ap Gronow, a mid 15th century poet, of which we have only the 1674 translation by Evan Williams:

Horn Gwennan, brought to the Gele
To be given a square mast,
Was turned back to Afon Ganol's quay
For Madog's famous voyage.

Gwennan Gorn, a legendary ship of Welsh folklore, is sometimes said to have been built by Madog for this voyage, and his departure from the Gele, at Abergele, occurs again in the version of the Madog story told by Sir Thomas Herbert in 1638.

It must be said that Abergele and the Afon Ganol are not the only places Madog left from, in the copious body of legend about him. When William Alexander Madocks dammed the Glaslyn and drained and reclaimed the land which had been its estuary, in the early 19th century, he called the village he then built there Tremadog, not after himself (or so he claimed) but because there was a local tradition that Prince Madog set sail for America from an island called after him Ynys Fadog, more or less in the middle of the land he had brought into being, now to be seen in the form of a hump in a field near the church.

These various starting points do not conflict with the story, let alone undermine it, since in the fullest version, as we shall see, Madog made two voyages. It would seem from the scrap of verse that the original setting out from Abergele was curtailed by storm, and we know from the court case that the Afon Ganol was a refuge in rough weather. The walling there is thought by antiquarians to be very old, possibly Roman, and the port it indicates may well have been one of some importance. It fell out of use only gradually, with the silting caused by the accretion of wind-blown sand.

By the time that Herbert wrote, the story that Madog sailed for America was well established. He was able to write conclusively that "Madoc ap Owen Gwyneth discovered America above three hundred yeeres before Columbus..." It was not, at the time, controversial to state this.

We have to see the sudden interest in Madoc during the 1580's in the context of Sir Humphrey Gilbert's two voyages to America in the autumn of 1578 and the summer of 1580. Gilbert, like his half-brother Sir Walter Raleigh, was a keen promoter of the proposal for an English colony in America, and although at first the programme failed, and Gilbert's ship was lost on the return voyage from annexing Newfoundland in 1583, enough important courtiers were putting the arguments to Elizabeth for the matter to have become a political issue.

Thus Madog appears in print for the first time in the Preface to Sir George Peckham's True Reporte, dated 12th November, 1583, although his first public appearance seems to have been in an oral presentation to the Council at court by Dr John Dee, on 3rd October 1580. What he said is summarised for us in the records: "The Lord Madoc, sonne to Owen Gwynedd, Prince of Northwales, led a Colonie and inhabited in Terra Florida or thereabowts". This, he explained, gave Britain the title to "all the Coasts and Islands beginning at or about Terra Florida... unto Atlantis going Northerly".

Peckham's 'Report' was an essay arguing the case for colonisation, and it sought to show that Britain had a rightful title to the Americas:

> ...it is very evident that the planting there shall in time right amplie enlarge her Majesties Territories and Dominions (or I might say) restore to her Highness auncient right and interest in those Countries, into the which a noble and worthy personage, lineally descended from the blood royall, borne in Wales, named Macock ap Owen Gwyneth, departing from the coast of England, about the yeere of our Lord God 1170 arrived and there planted himselfe, and his Colonies, and afterward returned himself into England, leaving certaine of his people there, as appeareth in an auncient Welch chronicle.....

It was perhaps Dee, whose parents were Welsh, who had introduced into the political situation at court the fertile theme drawn from an 'ancient Welsh chronicle', that America was first discovered by the Welsh. He would have been aware that the Tudor monarchy could itself claim to be the legitimate heirs of the kings of Gwynedd. Dee's prodigious learning certainly embraced the works of his countryman and elder contemporary Humphrey Llwyd, and it was this overlap in Dee's career which forms the bridge by which Madoc entered Elizabethan politics.

These people did not of course invent the whole thing there and then for their political purposes. Peckham referred to "an auncient Welch Chronicle", and we may confidently trace the origins of 16th century knowledge of Madog to Humphrey Llwyd's 1559 translation of the Welsh chronicles. This was published in an edition by Dr. David Powel, the personal chaplain to Sir Henry Sidney, in the form of his *Historie of Cambria*, in 1584. Here we now have the full story, with what became the standard elements, the background of civil war in Wales and the two voyages:

> Madoc another of Owen Gwyneth his sonnes left the land in contention betwixt his brethren, and prepared certain ships with men and munition, and sought adventures by seas, sailing west, and leaving the coast of Ireland so far north, that he came to a land unknowen, where he saw manie strange things. This land must needs be some part of that countrie of which the Spaniards affirm themselves to be the first finders.... And after he had returned home and declared the pleasant and fruitfull countries that he had seene without inhabitants; and upon the contrarie part, for what barren and wild ground his brethren and nephews did murther one another: he prepared a number of ships, and got with him such men and women as were desirous to live in quietnes, and taking leave of his friends tooke his journie thitherward againe.

Although this report from Llwyd via Powel is the version through which Madog's epic adventure came to be regarded as official history, and so, for instance, included in Richard Hakluyt's *Principall Navigations* of 1600, and prominently featured in Sir Thomas Herbert's 1638 edition of his book about his travels, it is not, of course, the earliest traceable mention of the matter. If it were it would be easy to dismiss the whole thing as convenient anti-Spanish propaganda, coming as it does at the height of the wars with Spain and only a few years before their culmination in the Armada. All this moreover is in the light of the colonisation of America by the Spanish and the knowledge of the voyage of Columbus. There are, however, indications that stories of a Madog who was a famous seafarer were popular some decades before Columbus sailed.

Powel added to his publication of Llwyd's account that on the second voyage Madog "went thither againe with ten sailes, as I find noted in Gutyn Owen". Since the latter wrote between the 1470's and the late 1490's it is possible, though not certain that his reference to Madog (which has not survived) was written before Columbus brought news of America to the people of Europe. Since we do not know what exactly Gutyn Owain said, we cannot even surmise how significant this would be. A slightly earlier reference (which Gutyn Owain appears to have copied) does indicate that something was known of Madog before the 1490's.

Hakluyt, in his *Principall Navigations*, cites a poem by Maredudd ap Rhys, which was probably written abut 1440. It contains two references to 'Madoc the bold', a son of Owain Gwynedd, including what appears to be a telling passage:

Madog wyf i'm oed, ei gais
Ar foroedd hyn arferais

I am a Madog to my age, and to his passion for the seas have I been accustomed. This is fairly taken to be indisputable evidence that at least by the middle of the 15th century there existed in Wales a tradition of someone called Madog who was a notable sea-farer. Perhaps, we might guess (going on this scrap of evidence alone) a figure like a folk-hero, Madog the sailor.

It must of course be noted that although this is undoubted evidence for a cult of Madog before Columbus, it is not of such interest as might at first appear. There is no mention of the discovery of unknown lands, let alone of America. A 15th century cult of a seafarer does not, in itself, imply exploration.

We do not, in fact, have any version of a Madog discovery before the 16th century. Much is made of the claim by a Flemish minstrel to have written a work called *Madoc*, but since we have not got the work we do not know what he said in it. This is a pity, because Willem, who wrote a work which has survived called *Reynard the Fox*, wrote about 1270, and so within a hundred years of the supposed epic voyage. Willem refers to himself as 'the author of Madoc', as if this were a better-known work than *Reynard*. It is proof, as Gwyn Williams, normally sceptical, puts it in his *Madoc, the making of a myth*, that "some story about Madoc a seafarer" entered "European literature during the thirteenth century".

Since it is also certain that such a story remained popular in the 15th century it is no surprise to find it being put to use in the 16th and referred to still in the 17th. The fact that his discovery of America (as opposed to his connection with the sea, and then his travelling to unknown lands) became explicit in the context of the British-Spanish wars does not of course prove, or even imply, that Madog did not discover America. For him to have done so, however, he would first of all have had to exist. What evidence, we may now ask, is there for that?

who was madoG?

"In the authentic medieval chronicles, prose and verse of Wales which survive, there is *not a single trace* of a Madoc who found America, a Madoc who sailed to distant lands or even a Madoc who was the son of Owain Gwynedd (though he might have figured in Owain's *teulu*, a word meaning warband or retinue which today means family, or among the imposing ranks of Owain's multitudinous bastards)." So writes Gwyn Williams, author of the last full-length work on the subject, *Madoc, the making of a myth.*

We know quite a lot about Owain Gwynedd, his reign, his life and times, and his sons. He came at the end of a turbulent period of Welsh history, and himself formed the start of a more settled one. To get this into perspective we need to go back a hundred years.

In 1039 the kingdom of Owain's grandfather was seized by the rival Deheubarth line, from south-western Wales, descended from Hywel Dda, the ruthless Gruffudd ap Llywelyn killing in battle Iago, the king of Gwynedd, his distant cousin. Gruffudd became thus king of all Wales, with English support. In the unsettled conditions of neighbouring England he even succeeded in regaining for Wales much of the Cheshire and Shropshire borderland. He handed over Gwynedd to be ruled by his half-brothers, and the heir, Cynan, survived by fleeing to Ireland.

Dublin was at the time the home of a settled Scandinavian colony, having been under Viking rule since the end of the 8th century. Viking raids were a persistent problem along the Welsh coast, as Irish raids had been in earlier centuries, yet it was not the first time that a king of Gwynedd had been forced into exile in Ireland. Cadwallon fled there from the invasion of Edwin of

Northumbria, in the 630's.

Cynan's time in Dublin proved to be of critical importance to northern Wales, since it fortuitously led to the end of Irish-Viking attacks and hence, in Owain's time, to a period when the Welsh could embark on their full-blown cultural history, writing down their traditions and their verse and building, for the first time in stone, their many churches.

This is all due to a rather surprising turn of events. Cynan became assimilated at the Scandinavian court in Dublin, to the extent of marrying Rhagnell, the daughter of the king. His son, Gruffudd, who was only eight when Cynan died fighting the English king Harold, was brought up in Dublin by his mother, more Viking than Welsh.

Gruffudd ap Cynan, accompanied by a probably rowdy horde of Vikings, made several attempts to return to his kingdom, and successfully ruled it again from 1081. He was briefly forced to return to Ireland in 1098, but returned the next year and remained in Gwynedd until his death in 1137, at the then remarkable age of eighty-two. He handed over to his son and heir Owain a stable and prosperous kingdom.

Owain was also fortunate that the beginning of his reign was a time of turmoil in neighbouring England, sometimes known as 'the Anarchy', when the king, Stephen, virtually lost control of parts of his country. The Marcher lords gained considerable independence from the Crown, but with it lost the benefit of the military support of the king. Owain was able to expand towards Chester, and also successfully spread his power into Powys. When Stephen was succeeded by Henry II in 1154 Owain's ambitions were checked, but he was later able to take advantage of the difficult position the king put himself in during his long-drawn-out quarrel with Thomas Becket.

Owain died in the same year as Becket's murder, 1170. The succession was this time unclear. His eldest son, Iorwerth, nicknamed Drwyndwn, was, the chroniclers tell us, passed over because of his deformity – Drwyndwn means 'flat-nosed', and evidently the ability to reign was considered impaired by the accident of, perhaps, a broken nose.

Among the other sons it seems the most ruthless was Dafydd, who took Gwynedd by force. He 'expelled from it all his brothers and all his uncles', we are told. That was in 1174, in which year he also 'seized Maelgwn, his brother, and imprisoned him'. Maelgwn had, in 1173, prudently fled to Ireland, when Dafydd took possession of the island of Anglesey, but evidently was rash enough to return. In 1170, the year of his father's death, Dafydd had started this career by killing Hywel ab Owain, his elder brother. His brother Iorwerth and his family were not in the meantime idle. In the course of a quarrel with the Lord Rhys, ruler of Deheubarth, he invaded and burnt Caerleon, and in 1175 his son Hywel 'unknown to his father, seized Owain Pen-Carn, his uncle. And after gouging his eyes out of his head he had him castrated lest he should beget issue who might rule thereafter over Caerleon'. That same year Dafydd continued his business: 'And then Dafydd ab Owain seized through treachery Rhodri ab Owain his brother by the same mother [and] the same father as he, and he imprisoned him in strait shackles for seeking from him a portion of his patrimony... And then Rhodri escaped from the prison of Dafydd, his brother; and before the end of the year he expelled Dafydd from Anglesey and from Gwynedd until he came across the river Conway.' Finally Iorwerth's son Llywelyn (later to be known to history as Llywelyn Fawr – *the Great*) with his uncle Rhodri and two cousins ganged up against their vicious uncle Dafydd and 'expelled him from all his territory except for three castles', in 1194.

One might feel that with all this going on in Wales America was much the better place to be. History does indeed authenticate the turmoil which forms the background, and motive, to the Madog story. The only trouble is that the voyage is supposed to have taken place in 1170, and most of the events which form this sequence take place after that, in fact during the next twenty or so years. We might suppose perhaps that Madog saw it coming; we might speculate that after the initial killing by Dafydd of his elder brother Hywel, Madog was taking no risks, and when he came back – the story does not say how soon – he found the family fighting to be so intense that he filled his ships with peace-loving people and left again at once. There is a further difficulty however, with the 1170 date. Owain Gwynedd died on 28th November. This does not leave Madog much time (even if navigational considerations favoured an autumn voyage, which one doubts), to experience the hostile situation in the aftermath of his death, to build and fit out the Gwennan Gorn, to set sail from Abergele and put in, stormbound, at Rhos on Sea, and to land in Mobile Bay the same year.

Giraldus Cambrensis, Gerald de Barri, who was alive at the time and wrote his *Itinerarium Kambriae* less than twenty years later, says that Owain "had many sons, but only one legitimate, namely Iorwerth Drwyndwn, which in Welsh means 'flat-nosed'… " One of the great doubts cast over the Madog story is that Gerald does not mention it, or him, though he was supposedly his contemporary.

It is said in excuse of this that Gerald was only twenty-four at the time, in 1170, and that between the years 1166 and 1172 he was at university in Paris. One would have thought however that by the time he came to write his detailed description of Wales, following his journey through it in 1188, he would have got to hear about the epic voyage and therefore mentioned it in the context of the succession to Owain Gwynedd, or in relation to the coastline of northern Wales.

Gerald's editor (Sir Richard Colt Hoare) adds a footnote: Owain Gwynedd "left behind him manie children gotten by diverse women, which were not esteemed by their mothers and birth, but by their prowess and valiantnesse". In fact what happened was that Owain married twice, firstly to Gwladus, by whom he had the sons Iorwerth and Maelgwn. He then married again to Christina, his first cousin, by whom he had Dafydd and

Rhodri. Because first-cousin marriage was considered to be incestuous the second marriage was considered invalid, and the latter pair of sons therefore illegitimate. Owain had at least six other sons by other women, including Hywel and Cynan. If Owain Pen-Carn, uncle of Hywel ap Iorwerth, was one of them, then the chronicles actually mention a total of seven: Dafydd, Hywel, Maelgwn, Cynan, Owain and Rhodri.

The chronicles were Welsh translations of a lost Latin text, *Cronica Principum Wallie*, and were written, probably by monks, during the late 13th century. They recount Welsh history from the death of Cadwaladr in 682 and stop, presumably because it was not known what came next, in the year 1282. That was, of course, the year of the death of the last Llywelyn and the end of Wales's independence. There are three slightly different versions, the two main ones being in 14th century manuscripts known as the Peniarth and the Hergest, from the places which housed the collections of which they formed part. They are published by the University of Wales under the title *Brut y Tywysogyon*. I have quoted above from the Hergest version, but there are no significant differences in the others for the passages which concern us. The striking point is that none of the chronicles mention Madog. When Dr David Powel published Humphrey Llwyd's translation of an ancient Welsh chronicle (Llwyd having died before he could publish), and in doing so launched the Madog story into the world, he compared Llwyd's work with manuscripts which appear to have been these of the chronicles. But Llwyd evidently had access to another original, and it was there, as it was definitely not here, that he found Madog.

Richard Deacon is of the opinion that ten Madogs are known of in Wales in the 12th century, but that none of them were sons of Owain Gwynedd. There are, he says, six of these Madogs who might conceivably be confused with a son of Owain Gwynedd. Three of them were rulers of Powys, and so princes. These are comparatively well known, in their own right. Madog ab Gruffydd, for instance, the son of Angharad, Owain's daughter, and so his grandson, ruled Powys from 1197 and died in 1236, being buried at Valle Crucis. He therefore did not end his days in America. Madog ap Llywelyn, who launched a rebellion early in the 13th century, can similarly be ruled out as being in Wales at that time, not America. Madog ap Maredudd, another prince of Powys, was related to Owain Gwynedd through marriage and is of the right date. He ruled Powys from 1142 to 1160, but his life is fully documented, and anyway he died in 1160.

There is a Madog mentioned in literature who may perhaps have given rise to the confusion, since he was a member of Owain Gwynedd's retinue. The poet Cynddelw Brydydd Mawr, who flourished between 1155 and 1200, sang his praises – though he sang too of his patron, Madog ap Maredudd, prince of Powys. The confusion possibly arises from the use of the word *teulu*, which literally means 'family'. It was the term used by the independent Welsh princes for their bodyguard or warband, the household troops who travelled with the prince on his constant progress from *llys* to *llys*. If then Madog was spoken about as being a member of Owain's *teulu*, it is open to someone to interpret this as his being a family member, and so his son. And indeed Cynddelw's ode, written about 1169, is sometimes titled 'Teilu Ywein Gwynet'.

Deacon, though his book is entirely supportive of the authenticity of the Madog story, quotes E. D. Jones in conclusion, the Librarian of the National Library at Aberystwyth, writing in the Journal of the National Library in the summer of 1965: "There is no contemporary evidence of even the existence of Prince Madoc as one of the sons of Owain Gwynedd". Gwyn Williams, as one would expect, goes a step further: "Whether there was a real Madoc…whether he sailed and where he sailed if he did, Heaven only knows and now only Heaven ever will know."

three

on being discovered

Of all the disinformation taught us in our appallingly Eurocentric educational system, perhaps the one which packs the most errors into the fewest words is the statement that 'Christopher Columbus discovered America, in 1492'. This news would have come as something of a surprise, for instance, to the million or so inhabitants of Tenochtitlan, the sprawling megalopolis on the site of what is now Mexico City.

The Aztecs had ruled much of central America since the mid 12th century, replacing the Toltecs, whose sixty square mile capital of Teotihuacan lies some thirty miles to the north-east, built, it is thought, by an earlier but unidentified nation, itself replaced by the Toltecs early in our era. They themselves had migrated from Guatemala and founded the magnificent city of Tula in about 650 AD. We should remind ourselves that we were not building pyramids and temples ourselves at that time, or making elaborately fanciful statuettes out of stone and clay. Our 'Dark Ages' were not as benighted as the term implies, and we were in the process of developing Christiantiy. But the Toltecs were way ahead of us in terms of civilised refinement.

Somewhere around 1194 AD the Toltecs took over Chichen-Itza from the Maya, whose great civilisation had started to decline by the tenth century, possibly weakened by a persistent drought. The Mayas' golden age, one of the great flourishings of American civilisation, had lasted for some six centuries, from about 300 to about 900 AD. They are thought to have numbered about two million people at their height, and they left for us to view with awe the towering remains at Uxmal and Chichen-Itza, cities populated by 30,000 to 40,000 each, and a wealth of elaborate jade and ceramic art.

Elsewhere in the region the mountain-top citadel of Monte

Alban, which probably dates back to a previous occupation as early as 1000 BC, became the seat of the Zapotec nation between the 3rd and the 10th centuries, extending to some 25 square miles, until they were overcome by the Mixtecs in about 1000 AD. The Mixtecs themselves had become subject to the Aztecs before the coming of the Europeans. There were at that time, it is estimated, about three million people in central America, out of a possible total of eight and a half in America as a whole.

Before any of these events the people known as the Olmecs had perhaps constructed the first buildings at Monte Alban about 1200 BC, and moved down to Guatemala about 400 AD, leaving us with twelve mysterious stone heads, between six and ten foot high, which confront us with the paradox of their distinctly Negroid features.

When Columbus arrived the West Indies were populated by Arawaks and Caribs, up to a million of them on the island of Hispaniola alone.

Meanwhile further south in Peru the Inca dynasty, developing slightly later, had started to expand in 1438, extending by the time the Europeans discovered it over thousands of miles, from Ecuador to Bolivia and including parts of Argentina and Chile. Their capital of Cuzco is still a sizable town, and the fortified mountain city of Machu Picchu remained unknown to Europeans until 1911.

In northern America what is thought to have been a flow back northwards gave rise to a more nomadic culture which did not to the same extent leave us the evidence of cities and temples. It was a way of life based on hunting rather than farming, and as such focuses more on the movement of people than on their historical background. Thus we know that the Navaho and the Apaches came out of the Northwest to the Southwest in the 13th century; that the Cheyenne moved out of the wooded country west of the Great Lakes into the central plains as late as the mid-17th. The Sioux similarly moved from the Northwest to the area of the Mississippi, and when we first know any details of them, in the 19th century, they numbered at least 30,000.

It was not all movement. The Hopi moved into the area of Arizona and New Mexico before 1000 BC, and they are still there. They developed the so-called Pueblo culture, a pattern of prehistoric settlements, and those of them who still live in the squat villages perched on the edges of the mesas of the Arizona desert, some of which have been in the same place for over a thousand years, practise a form of agriculture known as 'dry farming', by which they somehow coax life out of the desert.

Where, one may wonder, did all these people come from? There is evidence of human presence in the Americas from at least 30,000 years ago. The Clovis culture (named after the town in New Mexico near where it was discovered) flourished between 12,000 and 10,000 before present. It was distinguished by a particular shape of spear-head, and is assumed to have been a hunting society. By about 8000 BC it is reckoned that the whole continent was populated by humans.

It is assumed, because of their distinctly Oriental features, that the whole of this extensive population originated in Asia. "Anthropologists do not know all they wish to know about when, how, or from where in Asia American Indians first entered the New World," Alice Marriott and Carol Rachlin write, in the late 1960's, in their book *American Indian Mythology*. There are, they say, no prehuman remains: *Homo Sapiens* was "the only humanoid species that has occupied the Americas". It was in fact always a New World. "Men had become one biological species before the migration began."

The traditional explanation goes like this. Some 20,000 years ago the amount of water frozen in ice sheets and glacier-fields reduced sea level to the extent of allowing land-bridges to form between land-masses. One such, known as the 'Beringia' land-bridge, crossed what is now, and was before, the Bering Strait, the strip of sea between Alaska and Siberia which separates the continents of Euro-Asia and America. The Strait was of course traversable before that across the winter ice, but when it became dry land it formed a highway for the migration of first animals and then the people who pursued them. The first groups who crossed, about 30.000 years ago, made little impact, as their routes south were still closed by ice. Some 12,000 years before present a Canadian ice corridor allowed hunters from Siberia to reach the gamelands of the American plains. By 10,930 BP humans had reached central America, and they pushed on through South America about 10,500 BP.

It must be said that more recent information casts some doubt on some of this. For one thing it is now accepted that not the whole of the population came this way. Marriott and Rachlin already recognised that "…the possibility of raft transportation from the Pacific islands cannot yet be discarded." Discoveries in caves in north-east Brazil in the 1980's revealed that rock-art was being practised before 30,000 years ago, which suggests that colonists had arrived by some means which avoided the ice-sheets then cloaking the northern sub-continent.

More recently both DNA tests and archaeology have suggested a more startling and controversial conclusion. The American 'Clovis' culture appears to be associated with a form found in Europe, not in Asia; and it is with Europeans rather than Asiatics that the DNA links of American Indians may be found.

The supposition is, if this is so, that hunters followed the walruses and seals across the ice-flows of the Atlantic, where there would be more food to be found at the edge of the ice than on land. Such a theory would fail to explain the undoubted Asiatic characteristics of the Indians of both north and south America. It would, however, mesh satisfactorily with the widespread myth of the 'White Founder', which is often used to support the Madog theory.

The Collao people of Bolivia, for instance, informed the Spanish chroniclers that there suddenly appeared from the south a 'white man of large stature' who had such power that they took him to be the Maker of all things. Such a figure is Viracocha, said to be an early member of the Inca people who emerged from Lake Titicaca . It was because he was envisaged as a tall white man that the conquering Spaniards were at first taken to be gods, multiple reincarnations of Viracocha.

In the Mandan ceremony commemorating an event in their early history a man comes into the village covered in white clay, so that he seems to be a white man. This, George Catlin explains, is part of the point: 'for their tradition says, that at a very ancient period such a man did actually come from the West – that his body was of the white colour, as this man's body is represented…' He was 'at one time the only man', and when he reached the Mandans he taught them their rituals. When he first came to them he came, significantly perhaps, in a 'big canoe'.

If there were primeval contacts between Europeans and the New World then evidently, by one of those strange lacunas that seem to occur in history from time to time, all memory of this had got lost by the time we start to have records. There was on the face of it no reason for Columbus to think the Americas existed. There had been rumours of finds and strange objects, such as carved timbering, found at sea. It was clear to Columbus and the handful of people interested what this meant. There was indeed land out there. It was Asia.

The reasoning went like this. The world was a sphere. That had been by then generally accepted. The significance of this for our understanding of its place within the heavens and the solar system had to await the reasoning of Copernicus and Galileo. It remained for Columbus to underestimate the size of the world and overestimate the size of Asia. With those two premises accepted it followed that the back of Asia lay across the Atlantic.

Marco Polo had travelled to Asia with his father between 1271 and 1275, a fact well known in Italy where he came from, and where Columbus grew up. That side of Asia was therefore known of, and the programme was, in the mid-14th century, to open up trade with China, ruled, it was known, by the great

Khan. The advantage of arriving from the east was partly that it was thought to be likely to be shorter. As far as the Spanish were concerned the route also had the advantage of outflanking Portugal, which had already acquired territories along the route the other way.

It was to Portugal, however, that Columbus came, and his arrival was (as so much in his story) something of an accident. He was on his way to England in 1476 when his small fleet was attacked off Cape St. Vincent by pirates, and he escaped to Lisbon. He evidently liked it, since he came back there from the delayed trip to England in 1479, married the daughter of a Captain in the service of Prince Henry the Navigator, and from his new father-in-law's speciality became interested in maps.

The King of Portugal was more concerned with accessing Asia by a route around Africa, which the Portuguese eventually achieved. The really amazing thing about Columbus's eventual voyage is that it took place at all. For seven years he put forward schemes, first to the Portuguese court then to the Spanish, then to both of them again, his plan constantly rejected as being impractical. He did not help himself by putting forward greedy and ambitious schemes for his own advancement. Through influential friends he had gained the ear of the queen of Spain, Isabella, but at the time she and king Ferdinand were preoccupied with the war against the Moors in their own country.

Granada fell on 2nd January 1492, and Isabella was able to turn her attention to the persistent navigator. By 17th April an agreement had been reached. He was off to Japan and Cathay, with a letter from the King of Spain to the great Khan.

Since it is often thought that the Madog story simply echoes that of Columbus, and the fact that no full version of it can be found before the 16th century means that it might be derived from that, it is interesting to see what parallels there are between the two. Firstly of course their reasons for leaving were quite different. Columbus went in search of wealth and for the benefit of opening up new trade routes for his masters. Madog went in search of peace, in flight from an unbearably turbulent world. They both planted colonies – Columbus leaving 44 men on Hispaniola, when he returned with the news of his discoveries in 1493. They both made more than one voyage, Madog returning with more ships and people after an unspecified time; but Columbus made in all four voyages across the Atlantic to the New World, and Madog, it is specified, only two. Columbus encountered numerous islands, and only on his third trip did he sail from Trinidad to the coast of South America, which he took to be more islands. Madog seems to have gone a different way, since he is reported as having put in at the place where he eventually settled, regarded by John Dee (who, with his learning and his access to old documents, may be regarded as a good authority) to have been the coast of Florida. Columbus quickly set up a governing authority and had reinforcements sent out from Spain.

As a result of that, and perhaps of the failure of Madog's earlier attempt at colonising, the whole of the two American sub-continents became claimed as Spanish territory. The legal form of this was embodied in bulls granted by the Pope, then Alexander VI. The same had been previously done with regard to Portugal's claims on the African coast. Spain was confirmed in its right to all lands discovered west of a line drawn 100 leagues west of the Azores.

It may be assumed that at that time a Papal Bull would have the standing of international law. It is equally clear that what had changed by the time that this was questioned at the court of Elizabeth I was that the Pope's word was no longer sacrosanct in Protestant England.

When the Spanish moved into the Americas they moved fast. The Aztec king Montezuma was captured by Hernando Cortes in 1520, and Cortes went on to conquer Mexico effectively the next year. In 1526 Francisco Pizarro similarly brought about the end of the Inca empire in Peru. By 1539 the Spanish were entering the South-West of northern America in search of the mythical province of Cibola, but found instead of seven cities of silver and gold the mud-hut villages of the Pueblo people. Fray Marcos de Niza nevertheless reduced these to obedience to the King of Spain and the Catholic church. In the same year De Soto invaded the Floridas, and in 1540 Coronado entered the South-West.

It was with this conclusive annexation as background that Madog was first enrolled in the heroic campaign by the British to take on the vast might of Spain. It was partly because, in the face of probability, this was in the end successful, that North America became in the end a British rather than a Spanish colony.

four

€aRly voyaGeRs

There were (says Samuel Eliot Morison, in his 1971 book *The European Discovery of America*) two main motives for the medieval westward journey. The first was to find 'the islands of the blest', mentioned by the classical writer Hesiod, the 'Happy Field surrounded by Ocean', as Horace puts it. The second was to find a sea route, as opposed to the now familiar land route, to 'the Indies', by which was meant China, Japan, Indonesia and India. The importance of this was due directly to the importance of spice, an additive and preservative which disguised the state of meat in the times before refrigeration. The Indies were also thought to be the source of rich jewels.

The first notion came largely from imagination. The idea of Utopia arises naturally from our congenital dissatisfaction with our real world. If the world of the blessed is not apparent here, it must be somewhere else, and there is a limit to where that could be. From our western seabord we see the horizon of the western ocean, where nobody has ever been, and conclude that it must be there. 'No evidence from the classical writers' (Morison quotes Justin Windsor as saying in 1889) 'justifies the assumption that the ancients communicated with America', and, he adds, 'nor has anyone since discovered such evidence.'

The people of classical times did travel outside their familiar Mediterranean sphere. An explorer from the Greek colony of Marseille in the time of Alexander the Great had reached 'Thule', one of the north Atlantic islands, and thus opened up knowledge of a distant world. It was known since the time of Pythagoras, the 6th century B.C., that the world was a sphere , and this was conclusively proved by Aristotle by observing the earth's shadow on the moon during an eclipse, popularised by the Platonic schools and taught in ancient colleges and medieval universities. There was therefore from the start no problem about the idea of reaching the Indies by the other route.

When we come to the early Christian settlements, and particularly to the sea-going monks of Ireland, it was not riches or spices that they sought, nor even the earthly paradise, but rather the purity of freedom from the temptations of the world. An anchorite (from the Greek for the verb to retire or withdraw) was a religious person who set up for himself a remote cell as detached as possible from the sins of the world. In Ireland (which had become Christian during the 4th and 5th centuries) this led to voyages to rocky outcrops and to the presence of Irish monks as far away as Iceland and the Faroes. Many of those who undertook these adventures have remained anonymous to us, but one famously has not.

The story of St Brendan's voyage is told in his 'imrani', a saga as popular in the Middle Ages as the Song of Roland or the tales of King Arthur. A hundred and twenty manuscripts of it have survived, three from the early 11th century. *Navigatio Sancti Brendani Abbatis*. Together with a contemporary 'Life' it tells us a certain amount about him, though as we shall see the main saga is full of fantasy and borrowed folklore.

St Brendan is reckoned to have been a real person, born in the last quarter of the 5th century, perhaps 484, near Tralee. He founded four monasteries. During his long life he made voyages to England, Scotland, Wales, and Brittany, in the company of his disciple Maclaw, who became St Malo. Brendan became the Abbot of Confert, Galway, by now over seventy. He was told by an old friend, the Abbot Barinte, that the latter's son Mernoc had found the Promised Land in the west. Brendan selected fourteen monks, built a ribbed boat covered with ox hides, that is, a curragh. Morison points out that 'smaller and less seaworthy vessels than this have crossed the Western Ocean in our own day.'

Brendan and his crew sailed northwards. The wind dropped after two weeks.

By forty days they were out of supplies, when they found a rocky island but without a harbour. They succeeded in landing three days later and were greeted by a dog, which led them to a town with a castle, still with no apparent human population. Like several characters in Irish and Welsh tales they entered the castle's hall which they found hung with jewelled necklaces and items of silver. A feast had been prepared for them, after which they spent the night there, re-embarking the next morning with supplies provided by the single human they encountered, a mysterious and silent being who was, according to the tale, the manager of the monastery where they had been guests.

During the ensuing seven-year voyage Brendan and his monks visited many strange places: an island of sheep, and one of birds; they were lost in fog, reached the island monastery of the Irish monk Aelle, sailed north into ice, saw a volcano and an iceberg, and various monsters. They did, it is said, reach the Promised Land, and eventually returned, by which time Brendan was 93.

All this is supposed to have taken place between the years 577 and 583. 'Brendan was a real person, and in my opinion his *Navigatio* is based on a real voyage or voyages, enhanced by Celtic imagination. 'Morison further points out that three centuries after Brendan's time the Vikings found Irish monks in Iceland. He rules out the supposition that the story tells of the discovery of America, but insists it was a step towards this. Brendan probably explored the Hebrides, the Shetlands, the Faroes and Iceland, and went possibly as far as the Azores. The search for Brendan's islands became a seagoing tradition. 'In that sense the *Navigatio* may be said to have stimulated oceanic exploration for nigh one thousand years, and to have been a precursor of Columbus.'

Geoffrey Ashe, in *From Caesar to Arthur*, says that details given in the 'Voyage' of St Brendan are hard to explain away as fantasy. He points to Norse documents (which we shall consider) as giving evidence for Irish inhabitants beyond the supposed north American Viking settlement of Vinland. And he cites the native American tradition of bearded white men in long robes. 'Mexican annals and archaeological evidence (evidence which has tended to confirm the annals) point to the pre-Norse era as the time of the white men's arrival.' This is a big claim to base on so fanciful a document as the Navigatio, and we must look further into the background referred to by Ashe.

In one of the Norse sagas (the *Landnamabok*) the hero, an Icelander named Ari, sails over the ocean to 'Hvitramanna Land', "which some call Ireland the Great", near Vinland. There is moreover a reference which bears resemblance to a detail in the Madog lore: natives visited by Vikings in America speak a language which seems to them to be Irish. There is of course, in the background of this, the strong Viking connection with Ireland, which they began to colonise in the late 8th century and which they had partly overrun during the 9th. But more significant, and less well-known, was the Irish presence in Iceland. When the Norsemen first arrived there, intending to colonise it, in the summer of 870, they found a community of Irish monks already there. This surprising fact arises out of a simple chain of historical causes.

Christianity was established early in Ireland, and we have referred to the adventurousness of its sailing monks. It was from the start notably a religion with such national characteristics. Above all there is a crucial distinction between the Celtic church, in these early days and possibly throughout history, and the church of Rome. Essentially Columba's foundation at Iona and Aidan's at Lindisfarne were monastic communities, in which the abbot ruled an egalitarian and independent body. The Roman church had been from the start hierarchical, centralised, and based on the diocesan unit: bishops, rather than abbots, governed. The essentially remote and close-knit monastic community must have seemed at the time untouched by the long reach of the power of Rome. A confrontation between the two, attitudes of minds as much as schools of thought, took place at Whitby in 664.

The Synod of Whitby was a complicated affair, ostensibly to do with the means of dating Easter but clearly much to do with the rival influences of Rome and Lindisfarne over the Northumbrian monarchs. It concerns us here because in effect Rome won, King Oswui agreeing to conform to Roman practices and getting in reward Papal recognition of his supremacy in England.

There were important consequences of this result for the Irish church.

Part of the result of the Synod of Whitby was an attempt to bring the Irish into line with Rome. Rather than submit to this a large number of radical monks set sail as refugees, during the late 7th and early 8th centuries, and came to Iceland. This rather inhospitable island had been previously uninhabited. This initial Irish monastic colony, once established, was joined by further Irish refugees from Viking raids on the monastic communities in the Faroes from the late 8th century. Possibly there were about 1000 Irish in Iceland when the Vikings came.

This essentially religious community, based on the Irish monastic requirement to be remote and left alone, could not survive the arrival of the aggressive Norsemen, who had come with the specific intention of colonising the island. All the Irish left within a few years. The question is: where did they go?

There is no reason to suppose that they did not go back to Ireland, or to the Faroes. But this would have been no solution to their problem, since both places were now in the thick of Viking raids and settlement. That, after all, was the reason most of them had left there in the first place. They could, it is speculated, have gone on sailing west. That would explain the implication of Irish in America, in the sagas, when the Norsemen first got there. It has, however, apart from that and the apparent detailed knowledge of the area in the legend of St Brendan, no other evidence to support it. It must be said that no

Irish artefacts of this time have been found in North America.

We know a lot more about the movements of their enemies, the Vikings. At a time before the use of compasses, with only the North Star and the noon sun to guide them, they sailed the Atlantic widely. They were in the Faroes and Ireland before 800, Iceland by 870, and around 985 they went to Greenland.

Their expansion was to continue. They founded their colony in Normandy in the 10th century, and by the 11th they had travelled as far away as Sicily.

Two sagas tell us details of the voyages to Greenland, which we may refer to for convenience by their English names, The Greenlanders' Saga (composed about 1200), and the Saga of Erik the Red, of the early 1260's. The first of these, importantly, recounts six voyages which appear to have gone beyond Greenland to 'Vinland'; the second only three.

Erik the Red had to leave first Norway then Iceland when banished from each after committing manslaughter in revenge in the course of family or personal feuds. It is to these misfortunes that the Icelanders owed the discovery of Greenland. In exile from Iceland he spent three years exploring the east and west coasts of Greenland, from 982. On his return Erik called it by this attractive name as a deliberate piece of misrepresentation, and the name has stuck. He thought that by giving it a pleasant name, rather than one which described its true nature as a land of rock and ice, he would encourage other people to go there.

That was in 985. In 986 a Norwegian trader called Bjarni Heriulfson operating between Norway and Iceland followed his father, who had been in the company of Erik the Red, to Greenland. The Greenlanders' Saga tells us of his journey.

It was Bjarni, sailing in fog west of Greenland, who is credited with the first European sighting of the coast of North America, probably Labrador and Baffin Island, but he did not land. His voyage and description of what he saw prompted Erik's son, Leif, to set out to investigate further. He borrowed

Bjarni's ship for the purpose. His father Erik would have gone as well, but he hurt his foot and took this as a bad omen.

It is two hundred miles from western Greenland to Baffin Island. It is surprising that no-one had reported going there before, but we have to remember that the Icelanders had only recently reached Greenland.

Leif first found a land of forests, which he called Markland. He then sailed south along the coast of Labrador, until he came to a land of vines, which he called Vinland. He landed and wintered there, in a mild climate. "There was no frost in winter, and the grass hardly withered."

These vines are a problem. It is clear that it is the grape vine that is referred to, the one which makes wine. Yet wild grapes have grown no further north than southern Nova Scotia during historic times, and they are not abundant north of southern New England. When Vinland is mentioned again in subsequent medieval literature, first by Adam of Bremen in about 1075, it is said that the King of Denmark "spoke of an island.. which is called Winland, for the reason that vines yielding the best wine grow there wild". In spite of this there have been several attempts to suggest that it is not the wine-grape at all that is referred to, but some other sort of berry. Professor Merrit L. Fernalf, for instance, professor of botany at Harvard, is cited by Morison as arguing in a 1910 paper that the Norse word vinber actually means wineberry, not grape.

The next voyage to Vinland which the Greenlanders' saga tells us of is by Leif's brother Thorvald. Leif had built houses for his overwinter stay, and Thorvald succeded in finding them and used them as a base. He too overwintered, and spent two summers exploring. It is now that we hear for the first time about the natives. Thorvald was mortally wounded by an arrow, died in Vinland and was buried on a headland.

More serious attempts to colonise are then recounted. Throfinn Karlsfeni, an Icelandic merchant trading between Norway and Greenland, took three ships and two hundred and fifty men and women, together with livestock. They too ran foul of native hostility, and returned after three years, bringing with them two native boys from Labrador. It is much debated who these natives were, whether, for instance, Eskimo or Indian, but of course we do not know.

What we may perhaps picture behind the dramatic narratives of the sagas is a habit of regular visits to the new-found hunting grounds of north-east North America, with semi-temporary bases, leaving such signs as the three cairns at Kingigtorsoag (an island off the west coast of Greenland). Several of the supposed pieces of archaeological evidence for these visits have proved to be false.

There is, for instance, the stone-built tower at Newport, Rhode Island. This is first mentioned in 1675. It is probably a windmill of the English colonial period, dating from about 1640. There is the Kensington stone, discovered in Minnesota in1898. Its runic inscription tells of the arrival of Swedes and Norwegians in 1362. It has long been recognised as a modern forgery made by someone not fully conversant with numerical and dating systems used in medieval runes. But there is, on the other hand, the archaeological dig at L'Anse aux Meadows.

This is a settlement discovered in 1961 by Dr. Helge Ingstad, a Norwegian explorer, and his archaeologist wife, in Epaves Bay, northern Newfoundland. It consists of houses built of turf, which Morison says correspond closely to the Norse dwellings earlier uncovered in Greenland. The settlement showed subsequent use by Indian tribes, and appeared finally to have been burnt down. Charred roof timbers yielded a carbon 14 date of 1000 A.D., plus or minus 100 years. There was no sign of planting or cultivation nearby, and the speculation might be that this was a Greenlanders' summer station. Ingstad estimated that the settlement would have been populated by seventy-five to ninety people. Morison is of the view that this, 'beyond reasonable doubt', is Vinland. This is the cluster of houses that Leif Eriksson built, and in which he and later his brother

Thorvald overwintered and made their base for exploration, in the late 980's.

There are other possible Norse sites in northern Labrador. On the whole Viking finds are consistent with sporadic hunting trips, but the detailed excavation of L'Anse aux Meadows shows it to have been the site of permanent habitation. If Leif found Vinland in the 990's, and Thorfinn Karlsfeni, who took a colony to Leif's houses and for a time traded from there, gave it up in the face of trouble with the natives in perhaps about 1012, then the Norsemen were here on and off for not much more than a decade. Vinland was then lost, though not forgotten, for some time.

The name became generalised to refer to the coast of North America, though distinct from Markland which lay to the north of it, and was used in the sagas to refer to lands lying to the west of Greenland. Ari Thorgilsson, author of the *Landnamabok*, or Book of the Settlers, written about 1122, is the first Icelandic writer to mention the place by name, in his *Islendingabok*, the 'Book of the Icelanders'. It is possible though not certain that the name appeared once, perhaps twice, before that: once on a doubtful runic inscription from Honen in Norway, dated to about 1050 but now lost, which may have borne a reference to UINLAT, perhaps decipherable as Wine Land. Seconldy we have the word of Adam of Bremen, principal of the cathedral school at Bremen, who claimed to have heard of Vinland from Sveinn Ulfsson, King of trhe Danes from 1068 to 1076, which also would predate Ari's mention of it. Ari's account is our first certain authentic reference .

He heard of Vinland, he says, from his uncle, Thor Gellison, who got the information from a companion of Erik the Red on his expedition to Greenland. "Both east and west in the country" (that is, Greenland) "they" (the Icelandic colony) "found human habitations, fragments of skin boats and stone implements from which it was evident that the same kind of people had been there as inhabited Vinland whom the

Greenlanders call Skraelings."

Vinland occurs again in a 13th century chronicle, which gives an entry in the Icelandic annals for 1121 to the effect that Bishop Erik Gnipsson set out 'to find Vinland', but was, it appears, never heard of again. Vinland had in effect by then disappeared.

That remained much the case in fact until the name startlingly re-emerged in 1965.

The British Museum and Yale University had spent five years producing for publication a volume of medieval documents which included the apparently revolutionary parchment known ever since as the Vinland Map. Since this was sandwiched between undoubtedly authentic medieval parchments, with matching wormholes running through the whole set, it was judged to have been drawn in about 1440. The significance of this is that it showed Greenland, Vinland and Markland, saying in a marginal note that Vinland was discovered 'by the companions of Bjarni and Leif'.

The next year, 1966, an international conference on the subject of the Vinland Map was held at the Smithsonian Institute, though the Proceedings were not published until 1971. By then the map had conclusively been shown to be a forgery.

Spectrographic analysis of the ink with which it was drawn had shown that it contained a chemical called anatase, a form of titanium not available before the First World War. The analysis was published in Time magazine in February 1974. There are various versions of the explanation as to who made the forgery, and why.

Eric Wahlgren, in *The Vikings in America*, traces its origin to Luka Jelic, professor of history at the Catholic theological seminary in Yugoslavia, who died in 1924. He attributes to Jelic the rather hazy motive of revenge for the ignoring of his theories. The map then changed hands several times until turning up in New Haven Connecticut. Wahlgren claims to be able to identify the personal names on the map as being written by a southern European.

More recently it has been claimed that the map was made during the 1930's by Father Joseph Fischer, an Austrian Jesuit, who was an authority on old maps and hence had access to rare collections. Kirsten Seaver, whose interest is primarily in north Atlantic exploration, produces the results of eight years research in her book *Maps, Myths and Men: The Story of the Vinland Map*. She surmises that Fischer carried out the forgery as a reaction to the Nazi attempt to claim Norse culture as the progenitor of the Third Reich. Fischer (says Seaver) had got hold of a volume of 15th century manuscripts which had within it a blank leaf of parchment, genuinely dating from the 1440's. Seaver claims that the handwriting on the forgery is Fischer's.

Whatever may be the truth about the identity of the forger, it was undoubtedly Fischer himself who brought to light the Portuguese map of 1507 which is the first map to mark America by name. This, known as the Waldseemueller Map (now preserved in the Library of Congress) is of interest also as indicating that it was the Portuguese, and not the Spanish, who first explored the Pacific coast of the Americas. The Spanish did not cross the Isthmus of Panama until 1513, and Magellan (who was working for the Spanish crown) did not round the cape until 1519. Maps and charts earlier than the Waldseemueller map show the New World as being attached to Asia. The knowledge of its western coastline, shown by this map, is a crucial breakthrough.

There had been maps before that which showed a knowledge of a land somewhere out there. The Weimar map, dated at 1424, shows a land called Antillia, in the far west of the Atlantic; and a Genoese map of 1434 indicates the West Indies area as 'Isola Nova Scoperta', the newly-discovered island. These are no doubt the sort of maps being studied by the young Columbus, from his father-in-law's collection. It cannot be emphasised too strongly that whatever people might have thought when he came back, he did not go to find a new land but to seek a route past it. Hence when he found land he optimistically assumed it to be insular, as it almost all was, and tried to sail round it. He was not looking for a mainland, and it was partly for this reason that (unlike the Vikings) he took a southerly route. It is interesting to note in passing that of course the matter looked quite different from the other side; recent investigations published in Gavin Menzies' book *The Year China Discovered The World*, indicate that the Chinese navigator Zheng He took a fleet to America in 1421.

Unlike Columbus the Vikings who visited the western coastline in the North Atlantic were not looking for a passage past it. They were in the territory of the Atlantic cod, a fish which, capable of being preserved by salting, had enabled these long voyages in the first place. During the 15th century ships from Bristol were fishing cod off Newfoundland. It is their knowledge of that land's existence which inspired the next phase of Atlantic voyages, one which was perhaps more of an influence on the Madog theme than that of Columbus.

Giovanni Gaboti was born in Genoa about 1451, in other words in the same year and the same city as Christopher Columbus, raising the distinct possibility firstly that they knew each other, and secondly that their later voyages of exploration might have been undertaken in a spirit of personal rivalry. By 1484 he was in Venice, and possibly travelled from there to Spain. When he came to England in 1493 he became known as John Cabot, and it is with this name that he has been adopted by our national history. Cabot, like Columbus, was in the business of finding a quick and independent route to the spice lands of Asia.

The importance of spices – peppers, cloves, nutmeg – lay in their use for making unwholesome food edible. It may seem odd to us now that anyone should wish to do this, given the ability to preserve food by salting, but the level of effort and expense put into the development of the spice trade testifies to a value which we have to accept. Cabot came to England because it was at the end of the chain, far from the overland spice roots. He came to Bristol because that city was already sending expeditions into the Atlantic. We should see the British position as being the background to the eventual Elizabethan competition with Spain for the Americas. Henry VII had missed the opportunity to get a British toehold in the Indies. The Spanish and the Portuguese now controlled the two routes to (they thought) Cathay. He issued Cabot with letters patent empowering him to fit out five ships, in March 1496.

In the end only one sailed, the Matthew. Cabot was backed by Bristol merchants, perhaps in search of new fishing grounds. One of the backers was the Sheriff of Bristol, Richard Americke (a name presumably derived from the Welsh, ap Meurig) who is a possible contender for the honour of having given America its name. In 1896 one Arthur Hudd found in the muniment room of Westmister Abbey the Custom Roll for Bristol, which showed that 'Amerycke' paid Cabot £20.

The scheme was part of what had become an annual expedition, from 1481, from Bristol to search for the island of 'Hy-Brasil', a legendary and fantastic place of sophistication and wealth. The fact that the Bristol merchants were willing to go on funding the search for this place rather indicates that it had already been found, then somehow lost again. A significant detail might be the fact that Bristol had early Viking contacts. From the late 10th century there were Norsemen in the Severn estuary, and Bristol then became the main port (instead of Chester) for trade between the Irish Vikings and England.

The clue that when Cabot did reach Newfoundland on 24th June 1497 he already knew it was there (though Columbus had gone the other way, south to the Indies) comes in a remarkable letter from John Day, written in the winter of 1497-8, apparently to Columbus himself. Day was a wine-importer operating in Bristol in the early 1490's who later settled in Seville. The letter was found in Spanish archives at Simancas in 1956, in a folder labelled "Brazil", by Dr. Hayward Kensiton, professor of romance languages at the University of Michigan, and published in the Hispanic American Historical Review in 1956.

Day was writing to Columbus (*El Senor Almirante Mayor*) to satisfy the latter's concern at the possibility of Cabot posing a threat to his rights. He describes the trip in detail (which is why we know so much about it) and in passing lets us, and Columbus, know that the Bristol sailors had already been there perhaps several times by then:

> It is considered certain that this same point of land at another time was found and discovered by those of Bristol who found *el Brasil* as you are already aware, which is called *Ysla de Brasil* and is presumed to be the *tierra firma* which those of Bristol discovered.

The general view is however that Columbus did not know of Vinland. Morison says: "Valiant efforts have been made to hook up Columbus with Ericsson in order to prove the Greenland and Vinland colonies to be the real start of a causal sequence, instead of the dead end that they actually were..." The fact is that after the last record in the Icelandic annals of a ship having been to Markland, in 1347, there is a strange silence on the subject throughout Europe. It is speculated that climate change in the 14th century led to the failure of Greenland's precarious agriculture, and a fall-off in trade between Greenland and Norway resulted. Morison points out also that walrus-ivory was replaced about this time by elephant ivory, brought by the Portuguese from Africa. Greenland was cut off, and no longer of any concern. Vinland faded into the mist along with it.

Henry VII referred to the country Cabot had found as "the new founde lande" and "the Newfounded Island", giving it its present designation. It is clear that Cabot knew that it was an island, not the coast of China, though he perhaps still believed that he was on the way to finding a route through to that land. Cabot in fact, succeeded by his son Sebastian, set in motion what became a British obsession with the idea of the North-West

Passage.

Cabot made a second voyage, which we may well compare to Madog's, since he did not return. He and his sons (according to the Milanese envoy Soncino) were determined at the time to make London "a more important mart for spices than Alexandria". They believed, Soncino says, that there was a land out there "situated in the equinoctial region where he thinks all the spices in the world have their origin, as well as the jewels". On the second voyage five ships left, intending to form a colony, in early May 1498. One put into Ireland in distress, and returned home. Cabot and the other ships were never heard of again. There was no report or rumour back, no evidence of a landfall. Cabot's end perhaps has this distinction from Madog's. No Indian tribes have been discovered speaking with a West-Country dialect.

welsh indians

The Reverend Morgan Jones originally came from Monmouthshire and emigrated to America in 1660, in reaction to the Restoration. As a Puritan he was one of the forerunners of the Welsh Quaker colony who some years later followed William Penn, the ill-fated founder of Pennsylvania, to the New World, after the religious crisis surrounding the possible succession of James, Charles II's Catholic brother. Morgan Jones was for a time the pastor of a Presbyterian church in New York State and subsequently became chaplain to a Major-General in Virginia. Thomas Lloyd, Penn's deputy, had been a contemporary of his at Oxford, and the two met up in New York in 1686.

Thomas Lloyd had, it seems, already heard by then of rumours of Welsh-speaking Indians. He had been told by a cousin back in Monmouthshire that during the 1660's a Welsh sailor on a Dutch ship had talked in Welsh with Indians somewhere between Virginia and Florida. That might have been the earliest report of the Welsh Indians; but Morgan Jones's is definitely the most remarkable.

The Major-General to whom he was chaplain took him, in 1660 (in later versions 1666), on a trip to South Carolina . They got there successfully, but after some months of waiting for further ships to arrive they found themselves short of provisions. Rashly, we may think, Jones with five others set off on foot apparently intending to walk to Virginia. In 'Tuscarora Country' they were captured by hostile Indians.

Lloyd was so struck by Jones's account of what happened next that he asked him to write it down and sign it, as a result of which we are able now to tell his story in his own words. They had been told that they were to be executed in the morning:

Whereupon, being something cast-down, and speaking to this effect in the British tongue, 'Have I escaped so many dangers, and must I now be knocked on the head like a dog?' an Indian came to me, who afterwards appeared to be a war-captain belonging to the Sachem of the Doegs (whose original I found must needs be from the Welsh) and took me up by the middle, and told me in the British tongue I should not die; and thereupon went to the Emperor of the Tuscaroras, and agreed for my ransom and the men that were with me......

He was taken to the town of the Doegs, where he stayed for four months, 'and I did converse with them of many things in the British tongue, and did preach to them three times a week in the British tongue, and they would usually confer with me about anything that was difficult to them...'

He offers no explanation for these remarkable events, and does not on the face of it seem to know the Madog story. It is hardly possible, of course, that he could really not know of it, so his failure to refer to it in itself casts doubt on the veracity of his tale. Jones offered to take anyone who wanted to go to see the Doegs, but as he had allowed twenty years to elapse between the experience and the telling of it one might wonder whether he would seriously be able to do so. His offer, in any case, was not taken up.

The Doegs are almost unheard of, and one would suggest that Jones had made them up, except that an account in 1673 made by an Italian (and so independent of Morgan Jones) does mention them.

The story was slow in catching on, but when it did it probably formed the basis for many similar ones. It reached the ears of the Celtic antiquarian Edward Lhuyd in the 1690's, too late for use as propaganda in that Spanish war, but was published again in time for the next one, in 1740, the war with

An old wall in the garden of Odstone, Rhos-on-Sea, is supposed to be the remains of the quay from which Madog left.

PRINCE MADOC SAILED FROM HERE
ABER-KERRIK GWYNAN 1170 A.D.
AND LANDED AT MOBILE ALABAMA
WITH HIS SHIPS
GORN GWYNANT AND PEDR SANT

A plaque in Odstone's rockery commemorates the departure.

Details of the old wall at Rhos

Churches such as these began to be built in stone in the settled reign of Owain Gwynedd.

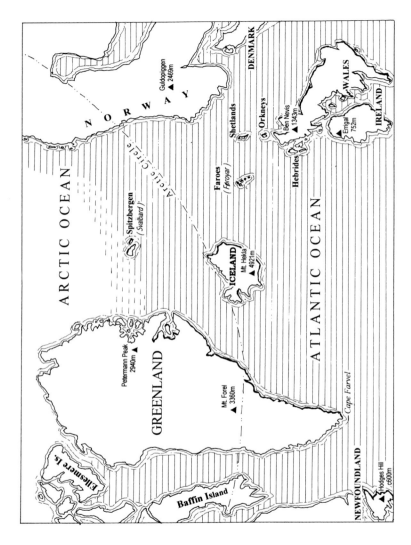

The Viking colonies moved west across the atlantic from Norway to Iceland, thence to Greenland

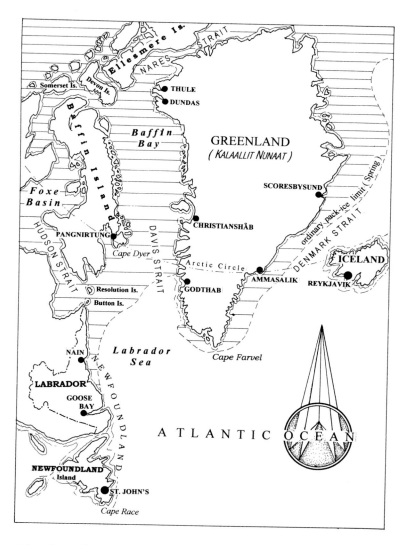

It is only two hundred miles from the west of Greenland to the nearest coast
of North America, Baffin Island

Dr John Dee was largely responsible for the rise of the Madog story at the court of Elizabeth I.

Ynys Fadog at Tremadog is another point from which Madog is supposed to have sailed.

Christopher Columbus

Christopher Columbus' memorial above Barcelona harbour.

L'Anse aux meadows in northern Newfoundland is the site of Norse settlement of about 1000 A.D. which was probably the legendary Vinland.

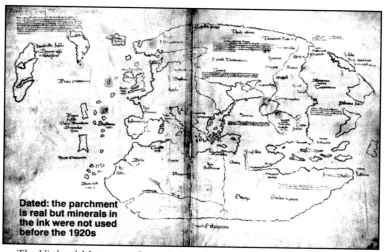

Dated: the parchment is real but minerals in the ink were not used before the 1920s

The Vinland Map, now shown to be a forgery, was for a time thought to prove the Viking discovery of America.

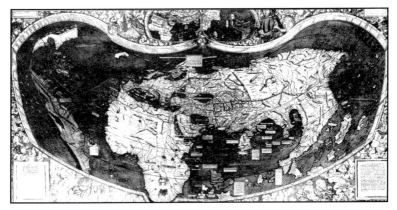

The Waldseemueller map of 1507 shows, for the first time, the Pacific coast of America.

The voyages of John Cabot, rivalling Columbus, lie in the background of the Madog story.

George Catlin (painted here by William Firk) lived for a time with the Mandan Indians.

Catlin drew the Mandan and wrote about their way of life.

English.	Mandan.	Welsh.	Pronounced.
I	Me	Mi	Me
You	Ne	Chwi	Chwe
He	E	A	A
She	Ea	E	A
It	Ount	Hwynt	Hooynt
We	Noo	Ni	Ne
They	Eonah	Hwna *mas.*	Hoona
		Hona *fem.*	Hona
Those ones	Yrhai	Hyna	
No, or, there is not	Megosh	Nagoes	Nagosh
No		Nage	
		Nag	
		Na	
Head	Pan	Pen	Pan
The Great Spirit	Maho peneta	Mawr penaethir*	Maoor panaether
		Ysprid mawr†	Uspryd maoor

*To act as a great chief—head or principal—sovereign or supreme.
†The Great Spirit.

James Girty, and later Catlin, claimed to detect similarities between the Mandan language and Welsh.

English	'Welsh-Indian'	Welsh
I	Me	Mi
You	Nehi	Chwi
He	Efo	Efo
She	Ea-ah	Hi
We	Noo	Ni
Water	Duah	Dwr
Bread	Bara	Bara
River	Nant	Nant
Father	Taid	Tad
Cow	Buch	Buwch
Partridge	Cluga	Clugjar
Woods-men	Coedig	Coed-wig
stone	kraig	carreg
old	hen	hen
dance	dansio	dawnsio
valley	koom	cwm (koom)
morning	borrah	bore (borra)
night	nostogr	nos
thanks	dyawf	diolch
I am	yr-effi	yr wyfi
He is	ym-eff	y mae ef
You are	Yor-iddich-ni	yr ydych chwi
in the boat	in y kook	yn y cwch
blue	glas	glas
milk*	faeth	llaeth
to cross	croesi	croesi
harp	tefyn	telyn
to be born	genni	geni
bridge	pont	pont
estuary	aber	aber
high	uchaf	uchel
to belong	pertin	perthyn
great	mawr	mawr
foot	troed	troed
disgusting	ake-e-Vee	Ach-y-fi
beautiful	prydfa	prydferth
sing	canu	canu

Today Waunfawr is a strung-out roadside village.

In John Evans's time Waunfawr was a small collection of farms.

Dafydd Ddu Eryri's illustration and bardic chair at Antur Waunfawr.

Iolo Morganwg

'General' Bowles was a colourful character in late 18th century London who claimed to be an Indian chief.

The Rev. Samuel Jones was regarded as the leader of the Welsh community in Philadelphia.

George Catlin's painting shows the highly distinctive form of a Mandan village.

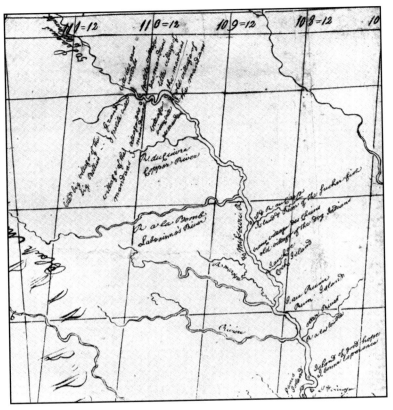

A part of John Evans' map showing the Mandan villages.
(Congress Library, Washington D.C.)

William Clark, who went to the Mandans after Evans, made use of his maps.

John Sevier, governor of Tennessee, encouraged the search for Welsh Indians.

Fort Mountain, Georgia, has been said to resemble Welsh hillforts.

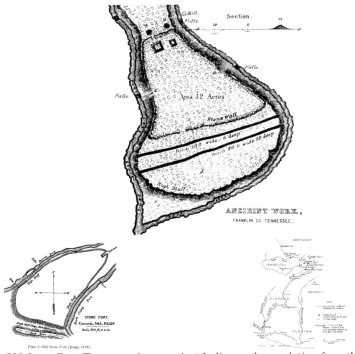

Old Stone Fort, Tennessee, is an ancient Indian enclosure dating from the 1st centuries AD.

Castell Dolwyddelan was supposed by one investigator to have the same layout as the ancient Indian forts.

In memory of Prince Madoc, a Welsh explorer, who landed on the shores of Mobile Bay in 1170 and left behind, with the Indians, the Welsh language.
Authority is - Encyclopedia Americana copyright 1918 - Webster's Encyclopedia - Richard Hakluyt 1552 to 1616, a Welsh Historian and Geographer - Ridpath's History of the World - ancient Roman coins found in Forts in Tenn. These Forts resemble the Forts of Wales of the 9th and 10th centuries and of the white Indians of the Tennessee and Missouri rivers.

The plaque commemorating Madog's arrival at Mobile Bay, Alabama, was erected by the Daughters of the American Revolution in 1953.

John Evans memorial at Antur Waunfawr.

An illustration of the Mandan Indians at Antur Waunfawr

Mandan craft at Antur Waunfawr.

John Evans' motto: "The Mandan tribe or death".
(Antur Waunfawr)

The 'fearless Welsh explorer's' story
on a commemorative poster at
Antur Waunfawr.

A Mandan village.
(as shown at Antur Waunfawr)

Part of the John Evans' maps exhibition at Antur Waunfawr.

Mandan craftware at Antur Waunfawr.

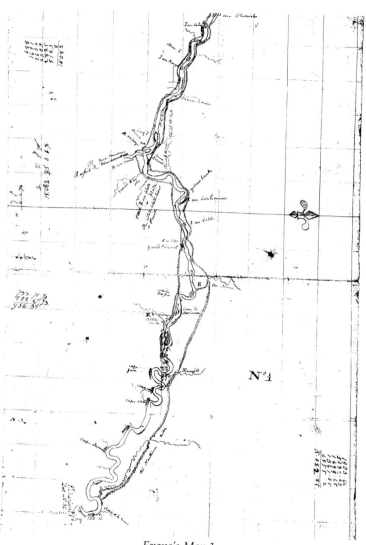

Evans's Map 1
(the Expedition's route about August 13-September 10, 1804)

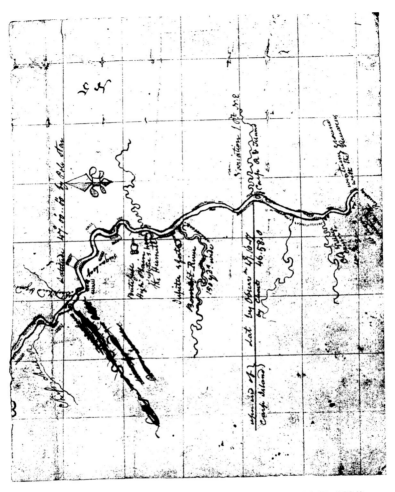

Evans's Map 5 (the Expenditition's route about October 14-22, 1804)
(John Evans' maps are reproduced by kind permission of

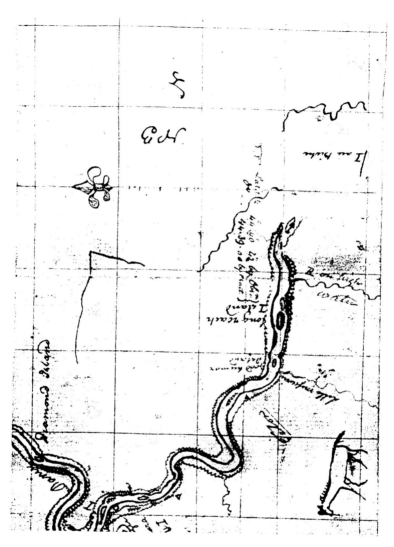

Evans's Map 3
(the Expendition's route about September 23-October3, 1804))

71

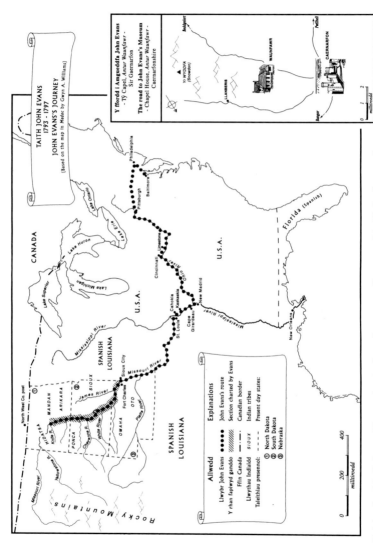

© *Map by M. Roberts. Drawn by Andrew Lawrence, Cartographic Unit, Geography Department, Keele University, 1998*

Spain known as the 'War of Jenkins's Ear'. It appeared in the second edition of Theophilus Evans's *Drych y Prif Oesedd*, in which Evans had told the Madog story in the David Powel version, appending the Morgan Jones one as evidence for it in his Preface. Two months earlier, in March, he had published the Morgan Jones story in *The Gentleman's Magazine*.

Once established on the continent of North America the idea of the Welsh Indians spread fast. Richard Deacon gives a list of sixteen quite separate areas where they are supposed to have been encountered, from British Columbia to Alabama, New York State to Mexico, and even Peru. Many travellers followed Morgan Jones in his extraordinary experience. All share his total lack of corroboration.

Not all the white-skinned Indians were Welsh-speaking, or claimed Welsh descent, nor were the Welsh-speaking Indians always white. Morgan Jones, for instance, did not mention a light complexion when describing the Doegs. Towards the middle of the 18th century, however, the two characteristics coalesce.

In 1755 a missionary called Charles Beatty investigated the story, and heard from an explorer called Benjamin Sutton of a tribe of Indians of a different complexion who spoke Welsh. Sutton introduces some elements into the story which seem familiar: the tribe had rites handed down from a founder 'who had escaped from a land far off after a battle between his brothers for possession of his father's lands'. They also had what appeared to be a Welsh Bible. Deacon comments: "The idea of Madoc taking Welsh Bibles into America centuries before the Bible was translated into Welsh, let alone printed, is so preposterous that one fails to understand how it was accepted by educated men."

In 1764 a Welshman called Maurice Griffith travelling with the Shawnee came with them to a village of white Indians. He addressed them in Welsh and was understood. Several other notably third-hand reports occur around this time of people meeting Indians who spoke Welsh. It is likely that the later 'witnesses' already knew the earlier stories. It is perhaps relevant that the late 18th century climax of such tales coincides with the London-Welsh revival of the 1790s.

The story meanwhile survived and spread. One remarkable incident was said to have occurred in 1801 in Washington. Lieutenant Joseph Roberts had cause to reprimand his servant in a hotel bar, and instinctively did so in Welsh. There was in the room 'one of those secondary Indian chiefs', who came over to him amazed (he said) that he was speaking his language. It turned out, says Roberts, that he 'knew better Welsh than I did'. The two talked for hours. His tribe, the chief told Roberts, lived about 800 miles south-west of Philadelphia and went by the name Asguawa. The explanation of the survival of their language was that 'they had a law or established custom in their nation forbidding any to teach their children another language until they attained the age of twelve years...' The tribe had a tradition that they had come from a far-distant country, very far in the east and over great waters.

Another outbreak of Madog sightings took place in the 1840's. In 1849 a company of Welsh Mormons made their way along the Mississippi and Missouri rivers to Salt Lake City. They were led by a Captain Dan Jones, from North Wales. Jones had had an interest in Madog's American descendants, apparently, since childhood, and in 1845 he wrote to Brigham Young giving details of reports of the proofs of their existence. For instance, "hunters and trappers of late years report having seen a tribe near the head waters of the Missouri River, speaking the Welsh language fluently." Young became interested himself, and in 1849 he sent Jones to look for these people. Jones wrote to a friend: "My mission is to search out that branch of the race of Gomer which are called Madocians; their story is well-known, and I go with the intent of bringing them into the fold of the Good Shepherd." And so he went to convert the descendants of Madog, still speaking perfect Welsh after more than six and a half centuries, to Mormon Christianity.

The expedition failed, and Jones was lucky to have survived it. Nevertheless he remained determined to find the 'Madocians', writing home to Wales of reports of white Indians speaking Welsh. He was about to be sent to look for them again by Brigham Young but the plan changed and he went back to Wales. There he made efforts to raise funds for further expeditions in search of them, which apparently failed. After 1856 Jones's correspondence does not mention the Madocians again.

All this took place of course in the aftermath of John Evans's epic expedition of 1792, itself the aftermath of Dr. John Williams's book of 1791. These critical events in the long saga of the Madog story are to be investigated in the next chapter. Further in the past background to this lie the visits to the Mandans, which began as early as the 1730's

The Mandans were the most easterly of the Plains Indians, once the dominant group of Upper Missouri tribes. They were a settled people who lived in old-established villages. Early reports of contact with Mississippi and Missouri Indians came from fur traders, and from such missionaries as the French Jesuit Fr Pierre Charlevoix, who was on the Mississippi as early as 1721. As a result of these rumours the French explorer Sieur de la Vérendrye set out in 1735 deliberately to search for the Mandans, who had even by then become something of a fabled presence outside the world by then discovered by Europeans. From him we have the first direct account of them, following his arrival in their area in 1738. The Mandans were rediscovered by a French fur trader, Jacques d'Eglise, operating up the Missouri in 1790. When d'Eglise reached them he said they were 800 miles 'from the city', presumably St. Louis, a population he estimated at 5000, 'a mighty and wealthy tribe of Indians' living in fortified cities, and 'white like Europeans'. Surprisingly when he reached them there was a Frenchman already there, married to an Indian woman and gone native, though it is not clear (apart from the name Ménard) who he was. The Lewis and Clarke expedition of 1804 also reached the Mandans, reporting them then to number 1250. The Mandans were of interest to both the fur trading companies by then in existence, the Hudson's Bay Company and the North West Company, and James Mackay, a Scotsman working for the latter, seems to have reached the Mandans in 1787.

We know a great deal about the Mandans thanks to George Catlin, because he lived among Indians, including them, for eight years in the 1830's, and particularly because he wrote such an entertaining book on the subject, *North American Indians*, more correctly *Letters and Notes on the Manners, Customs and Conditions of the North American Indians Written During Eight Years' Travel (1832-1839) Amongst the Wildest Tribes of Indians of North America,* which was published with his own beautiful illustrations, in Philadelphia in 1841 and in London in 1844.

Catlin was born in Pennsylvania in 1796, trained as a lawyer but instead became a painter, becoming successful as a portrait painter in Philadelphia. He had a life-long interest in the Plains Indians, and in 1831 began to visit the tribes. Thus in 1832 he came down from Fort Union at the Mouth of the Yellow Stone in Upper Missouri to land his green-timbered canoe at twilight in front of a Mandan village.

Catlin finds the Mandans strange from the start, unlike the other Indians. They describe themselves mysteriously as the "people of the pheasants", which is odd in itself, since there are apparently no pheasants in Upper Missouri. Catlin speculates that they were "perhaps one of the most ancient tribes of Indians in our country". Their origin, he says initially (it seems before he was made aware of the Madog story) is "involved in mystery and obscurity". They themselves claimed to be the first people on earth. By the time Catlin found them they had dwindled as a nation, having once been more powerful. Wars with neighbours had reduced them.

They were at that time resident on the west bank of the

Missouri River some 1800 miles above St. Louis, 200 miles below the Mouth of the Yellow Stone River. About 2000 of them, Catlin reckoned, lived then in two villages, to which they had moved within then living memory from fifteen or twenty miles down river. The villages consisted of the Mandans distinctive lodges, half-buried earth-covered circular huts formed on a substructure of timber with a smoke-hole skylight in the middle. Twenty to forty people of an extended family occupied each of the spacious lodges. They are, Catlin says, a cheerful people, chattering and laughing and playing games.

It is clear that in his initial perception of them he sees them as a tribe distinct in essential characteristics from other Indian tribes, yet as fully Indian as them: "There is really a newness and rudeness in every thing that is to be seen..." He certainly does not initially describe them, or anywhere depict them in his paintings, as having a pale complexion: "...the people are all red, yet distinct from other red folk I have seen." They have "an air of intractable wildness about them..." These perceptions he later modified, as we shall see.

Catlin's reports of their customs and rituals emphasise their complete contrast with European customs. Their behaviour in fact strikes both him and us as strange and savage. They do not bury the dead, but leave the corpses (with much ceremony) to decay on individual platforms raised on scaffolding just outside the village, "a great number of these bodies resting exactly in a similar way". Some hundreds, he says, attended by the mourning bereaved, who eventually place the bleached skulls of their loved ones in circles on the ground, where they come to converse with the dead and offer them food on an almost daily basis.

Catlin describes in detail the Mandans' exotic dress, which he compares with that of other tribes, and their manners and customs, always bringing to bear a careful objectivity. He does not judge, and resists all temptation to see the natives as in any way inferior, though he uses the word 'savage' to distinguish them from urbanised people. In this he is every bit a relativist – they might, he sees, find us equally odd, but would be too polite to say so: "An Indian will not ask a white man the reason why he does not oil his skin with bears' grease, or why he does not paint his body – or why he wears a hat on his head, or why he has buttons on the back part of his coat, where they can never be used…"

The Mandans' rituals strain this dispassion to its limits, but even while gasping at them with disbelief he struggles to maintain it. Catlin goes into lurid detail on the sequence of initiation rites beginning with the 'bull dance'. The ceremony "is truly shocking to behold, and will almost stagger the belief of the world when they read of it," he comments, with indeed some understatement. The rite of passage involves the young men being hauled to the roof of the 'medicine lodge' by a rope tied to wooden skewers passed through the flesh of their breasts. They later sacrifice fingers to the Great Spirit, and the final ordeal known as 'the last race' is something one would have thought it impossible to survive. Such behaviour, together with the wearing of buffalo skins and body-paint, buffalo masks made from the skin of the creatures' heads with the horns still on, and so on, does not immediately point to a relation to medieval Wales, and indeed such does not seem to have occurred to Catlin at this stage.

It might be mentioned here that the book takes the form of 'Letters', which appear to be his notes made day by day, which add new information as it becomes available to the writer, and hence have apparent contradictions in later letters of statements or impressions given in earlier ones. Hence he is able to back down slowly from the initial assertion that the Mandans were 'red'.

A stranger in the Mandan village is first struck with the different shades of complexion, and various colour of hair which he sees in a crowd about him; and is at once almost disposed to exclaim "these are not Indians."

There are a great many of these people whose complexions appear as light as half breeds; and amongst the women particularly, there are many whose skins are almost white.

At this point, however, he seems still not to have thought of a Welsh connection: "Why this diversity of complexion I cannot tell, nor can they themselves account for it. Their traditions, so far as I have yet learned them, afford us no information of their having had any knowledge of white men before the visit of Lewis and Clarke, made to their village thirty-three years ago." Their hair colour, he says, is also varied, and they have the peculiarity of occasional premature greyness.

Although the Mandans, in Catlin's description, show no sign of European influence, in their culture or behaviour, and in fact exhibit notably un-European habits, this does not stop him adding, at the end of the chapter in which he has finally left them, the suggestion (and he stresses that it is not at that point a theory) that there may be a Madog connection. He sees them as 'an amalgam of civilized and savage', far remote, though they are, from any possible civilising influence. It is in the absence of any explanation for this that he is disposed "to enquire whether here may not be found, yet existing, the remains of the *Welsh colony* – the followers of Madoc; who history tells us, if I recollect right, started with ten ships, to colonize a country which he had discovered in the Western Ocean; whose expedition I think has been pretty clearly traced to the mouth of the Mississippi, or the coast of Florida, and whose fate further than this seems sealed in unsearchable mystery." It is to these few words, later developed by Catlin, that the Mandans owe the start of their long-lasting identification with the people of Madog.

Catlin says that he will not put this forward as a theory rather than a suggestion without doing more work, and he evidently did some on his return, since the book contains an Appendix called The Welsh Colony.

In Letter 22 he promised not to return with this as a theory until "after I have collected other proofs, which I shall take great pains to do; after I have taken a vocabulary of their language…" Such restraint marks him as a serious anthropologist, and so gives us some confidence in his conclusions. By the time he added his two Appendices (the other being on the subject of the Extinction of the Mandans, and so we know written after he heard of the smallpox epidemic in 1838) he had evidently satisfied himself that he had done this work. It must be said, however, that the arguments he puts forward do not entirely stand up to the sort of rigorous scrutiny which he would have welcomed.

By Catlin's own admission the 'Welsh colonists' would have had to have changed very considerably to have become the Mandans, while somehow retaining "so many peculiarities in looks and customs". On the basis of fortifications in Ohio which, he says, are too advanced in form to be the work of 'savages', he posits a race which has been obliterated or absorbed. This, even if it could be proved, provides no link to Madog, and the fact that 'Mandan' *could* be a corruption of 'Madawgwys' does not in itself prove that it is. His reasons in support of this connection are no less tenuous. Though he convincingly traced the Mandans back to their former territory by the excavated foundations of their distinctive huts, the fact that they had moved over time up the Missouri River does not provide support to the idea that they came from Wales before that. Their name for themselves – 'the people of the pheasants' – he says with apparent reason indicates that they came from a country where pheasants existed, "which cannot be found short of reaching the timbered country at the base of the Rocky Mountains, some six or eight hundred miles West of the Mandans, or the forests of Indiana and Ohio, some hundred of miles to the South and East of where they last lived." This is to suppose that 'pheasant' is a correct translation, and it seems at once strange that a people should have a word at all for a bird which they have never seen. Even if it is supposed that they brought the word with them from far away, it is not clear how Catlin, or we, could tell precisely what sort of bird is being referred to.

The Mandans have an art of making blue glass beads, which for some reason Catlin thinks must have been taught them by 'some civilized people', though he does not go so far as to say that the making of blue glass beads was a habit in medieval Wales.

Perhaps the most compelling link with Wales is the Mandan canoe. We have to believe him when he says that these are "altogether different from those of all other tribes". There is also no denying that they are of the same form as the Welsh coracle: skin stretched over a willow frame, round like a tub, easily portable, paddled by one oar pulling over the front. If this is proof of outside contact, however, it could as well be enlisted to support the cause of St. Brendan, since all the same things could be said of the Irish curragh. It is common in any case to find diverse people, such as could not have had any common contact, reaching the same solution to the same problem given the same available materials at the same stage of development of their skills.

Elsewhere Catlin bases his conclusion that the Mandans had contact with Europeans on their ceremony involving the arrival of a man painted with white clay, "so as to resemble at a little distance, a white man", known as Nu-mohk-muck-a-nah, 'the first or only man'. Their tradition is that such a man in very ancient times came from the west – which is of course the wrong direction for this argument – and taught them the myth of the Flood, which involved the curiously familiar element of a dove bringing a willow twig. The Mandans had a cult object, a sort of ark, known as the Big Canoe, in which the first man had landed on a mountain as the flood subsided. He also instructed them in their rituals and ceremonies. Catlin concludes that the similarity of detail with the Biblical flood means that the Mandans had some contact with Christians, perhaps "that missionaries or others have been formerly among them". It is only later, when his attention had evidently been drawn to the Madog story, that he makes the Welsh connection.

By Catlin's own account the Mandans' belief in their origins (that they came from inside the earth) does not involve any long voyage or provide any clue about the cause of their unusual pigmentation.

Catlin produces a long list of words in Mandan and Welsh which appear to have something in common. The Mandan for the first person singular is apparently 'Me', which is undoubtedly similar to the Welsh accusative form 'mi' – but then it is even more like the English 'me', and no one is suggesting that the Mandans are half English. On the face of it the Mandan words in Catlin's list are no more related to the Welsh ones than might happen by chance: Mandan 'Noo', for 'We', is only loosely comparable to Welsh 'Ni'. The Mandan for 'head' is (he says) 'pan', which is certainly not unlike the Welsh 'pen'. Much presumably depends on how one hears and transliterates a non-literate language. Catlin's efforts to make the two conform undermine rather than strengthen his argument. 'Megosh', for instance, Mandan for some form of negative which Catlin defines variously as 'No, or, there is not', is not conclusively related to Welsh 'nagoes'.

In a letter on the subject written after returning to London Catlin revealed slightly more about how he had come to his conclusions. He says he found that Mandan "consists of a language within a language, and it would seem that the more ancient part of that language is cherished for certain special occasions and for certain functions of everyday life. Quite often I found that where there were two or more words with one meaning, one of those words would be the equivalent of Welsh. The Mandans themselves invariably explained that some of the

Welsh-sounding words had almost gone out of use."

There is some evidence of this falling out of use from a remarkable study made about sixty years before Catlin's observations by a runner operating between the British and the Indians called James Girty, during the last third of the 18th century. Girty it seems had learnt Welsh, though he was not of Welsh blood. His full list of comparisons was said to be of more than 350 words and phrases, though he had no information as to grammar. Some of his words are the same as Catlin's, though there are many that the later writer apparently did not know of. Some of the similarities are quite remarkable. The Mandan for bread, for instance, is said to be 'bara'. The Mandan for 'Father' is 'Taid', the Welsh for 'grand-father' and clearly related to 'Tad', 'Father'. 'Nant', 'hen', 'glas', 'croesi', 'pont', 'aber','mawr' and 'canu' all appear in exactly the same form, with the same meanings, in both languages, and others such as 'koom', meaning 'valley', and 'dansio' meaning 'dance' are only different in a matter of spelling.

There were at various times attempts to stretch the Welsh-American linguistic connection further, and Richard Deacon calls the identification of Curaçoa as being derived from 'Croeso' "a ridiculous contention on any grounds other than a faint phonetic resemblance". From Elizabethan times it was noted that there was in America a bird known locally as Penguin, which it was asserted was from the Welsh 'pen', 'head', and 'gwyn', 'white'. This is odd, says Deacon, since penguins have black heads. Deacon tellingly adds: "One must concede that there is no trace of Welsh in any Indian dialect today."

There remains the problem of the Welsh speakers who conversed with Indians. Coincidences are, Deacon says, no answer to their claims, "unless one dismisses them as liars, and there are too many of them to put them all in this category." It does seem possible, on the face of it, that the number of them is compatible with their having heard the tale told already, and in retelling it came to let it be thought that it had happened to themselves.

It is in fact almost inconceivable that traces of a language could survive for hundreds of years without any traces of the culture of which it would be the central medium. Had the Mandans retained elements of the Welsh language they would have retained with it, one would think, a tradition of their origins. Yet Catlin, who describes their lives in minutest detail, does not say that they had a foundation myth which has them coming from over the ocean. And Catlin caught them in the last stage of their natural condition, though depleted by war and by disease, and moved from their original homeland, in the 18th century.

Catlin left them in 1834. Three years later, in the summer of 1837, fur traders travelling up the river in the Fur Company's steamer arrived at the Mandan villages with two crew members ill on board. Perhaps they did not know then that it was small-pox. For some reason the Mandan Indians have a very low resistance to this disease, and it swept through their community with terrifying swiftness. They were unable to disperse into open country because the area they were living in was surrounded by Sioux, their traditional enemies. The spread of the disease was hastened by the fact that the dead were left unburied, perhaps because there was no-one well enough to bury them, but probably because the Mandans did not want to anger the Great Spirit further by departing now from the ancient custom of exposing the dead.

Catlin says they were reduced to thirty or forty people, others put the figure at 150. He thinks that was the end of the Mandans as a tribe: "...although it may be possible that some few individuals may yet be remaining, I think it is not probable; and one thing is certain, even if such be the same, that, as a nation, the Mandans are extinct, having no longer an existence."

The remnants of the Mandans were taken as slaves by the Riccarees, and later largely exterminated in a battle with the

Sioux. What then remained joined the Hidatsa when they moved from the Knife River area to the Fort Berthold trading post in North Dakota. In 1870 a large reservation was formed for the Mandans, Hidatsa and Arikara. This in due course was drowned in 1950 by the formation of the Garrison reservoir.

"As a matter of interest," writes Deacon, "the census of Indian tribes in 1946 gave the total number of Mandans still existing as 396, though it can be categorically stated that these so-called survivors cannot be considered either ethnologically, nor historically, as belonging to the original Mandan tribe." Gwyn Williams, with a film crew from the BBC, found some people who claimed to be Mandan, or half-Mandan, in the spring of 1976. There are some who call themselves Mandans still, though they do not bear the hallmark of white skin nor talk in Welsh.

SIX

Refutations

If the test (as Plato said) of whether something exists is that it should have an effect or an impact, then there can be no doubt about Madog. Maybe there was no such person, no so-named son of Owain Gwynedd. The effect of supposing that there was has however been so enormous that we have to take the idea, at least, of Madog, as being a highly significant reality.

One of the most prominent occurrences of his powerful influence was that imposed on the brief but eventful (indeed almost incredible) life of a boy from the village of Waunfawr, near Caernarfon, in Gwynedd. Waunfawr is, now, a long-drawn-out linear village, strung-out along the road which goes up towards Snowdon from Caernarfon to Beddgelert, via Betws Garmon, Llyn Cwellyn, and Rhyd Ddu. At the time we are concerned with it was entirely different. It was more of a collection of small-holdings forming a loose-knit hamlet. Something of the feel of this can be got from the older area off the road, where the Antur Waunfawr facility occupies land which once belonged to the Chapel where the Evans family prayed, where now there is a John Evans room housing copies of his important maps of the Missouri, outcome of the obsession with Madog which brings him into this story, a copy of a letter on the subject, and other memorabilia. Here one gets the feeling of a private world, set in a lush, intimate valley, stopped by the twin bulks of the mountains Moel Eilio and Mynydd Mawr.

John Evans was a member of a prominent Methodist family, born in Waenfawr in 1770. Both his father and his older brother were preachers, and it seems that the fervour of belief and the urge to spread it must be seen as motive forces for his strange and in the end fatal obsession. An influence on his thinking also very probably came from the poet David Thomas, better known by his bardic name of Dafydd Ddu Eryri, who lived in that village and may very probably have taught the boy John. Ellen Pugh, in her book *Brave His Soul* speculates (I think it is no more than that) that it was Dafydd Ddu who arranged for John to go to London, knowing of the plans for seeking the Welsh Indians which were at the time (June 1791) raging there. Since Evans later quoted from a poem of Dafydd's which won a prize at the Llanrwst eisteddfod in June 1791 it is also speculated (for instance by Gwyn Williams) that he was there, at Llanrwst, when it was read, and was inspired by it to undertake his brave mission.

Taenad goleu, tywyniad gwiwlon,
I'r gorllewinol gyrau llawnion;
Gwawr o ddiwygiad gywir ddigon,
Draw i Fadawgwys – drefedigion.

'Let there be light, a fine shine,/ to the wide borders of the west,/ a dawn of correct reformation/ as far as the land of Madog and his colony.' The poem was later published in *Cylchgrawn Cymraeg*, a magazine which only had a few issues, but which followed John Evans's journeys closely, in February 1793. It is actually in the form of an ode to truth, and is not, apart from the reference in the last line, a poem (as it is often said to be) specifically about the conversion of the Madocians. It is in style pompous and stilted, in the fashion perhaps of formal Welsh verse of its time. An explanatory note (apparently added by the magazine's editor) is perhaps relevant, as drawing attention to the Madog legend, though again this cannot have been an influence on Evans, since by the time of publication he had already gone. 'It is well known to many of us' (it reads in translation) 'the history of Madog ab Owain Gwynedd, the way he mustered many of his compatriots in the year 1170 and sailed away with ten ships across the western sea, bidding farewell to

Wales, in the hope that they would settle in a more peaceful and pleasant country: there is no doubt that those mentioned above are the forefathers of those living in America today.'

Though Dafydd Ddu's awdl does not in itself explain John Evans's sudden move to London, its assumptions are symptomatic of the thinking in Welsh intellectual circles at the time, that is, precisely, the summer of 1791. Another influence might have been that of the rabble-rousing William Jones, a poet and radical nationalist, teacher and antiquarian from Llangadfan in Montgomeryshire, who toured the country at this time exhorting the young people to emigrate to America to free themselves from the grip of extortionate landowners. Jones had become something of an expert on America, of which, to the Welsh of the time, Madog was an essential component. He was also at the Llanrwst eisteddfod, in June 1791, where he circulated a tract which quickly became an influence on the London-Welsh scheme to find the Welsh Indians. Waunfawr is not exactly near Llanrwst, and there is no reason to suppose John Evans was there when the address was distributed, though it may have come to him, of course, through Dafydd Ddu. So forceful is William Jones's use of the idea of Madog that it is indeed tempting to see in this manuscript the explanation for Evans's sudden move to London, and then to America, which otherwise seems to be entirely missing.

The tirade is addressed to 'All Indigenous Cambro-Britons'. It starts by announcing that the descendants of Madog have been found, and are living as a free and distinct people who 'have preserved their liberty, language and some traces of their religion to this very day'. The pamphlet urges the 'Cambro-Britons' to send 'a qualified person or persons' to communicate with 'our remote brethren' not just to satisfy curiosity, but with the aim of restoring full Christianity to the remnants of the religion they were supposed to have retained. Other benefits were suggested, such as trade, circumventing through the Madocians' independence the blocking by the Spanish of commerce beyond the Mississippi. The address brought nationalistic fervour and the bitterness of deprivation to the enterprise. 'Some modern sceptics have thought proper to deny that Madog never discovered America because (forsooth) they will not acknowledge that a Welshman is capable of performing any brave or generous action.' It was said by its author to have been well received at Llanrwst.

The ultimate source of the London-Welsh excitement was the publication by Theophilus Evans, first in the Gentleman's Magazine in March 1740, then in the second edition of his *Drych y Prif Oesedd* of the Morgan Jones story. A more immediate cause was the publication in 1791 of a book called *An Enquiry into the Truth of the Tradition Concerning the Discovery of America by Prince Madog ab Owen Gwenedd about the year 1170*, by Dr. John Williams, who had studied Madog lore for thirty years. This was, as it says, a review of all the material then available, and just as Theophilus Evans's letter can be seen as a response to the politics embodied in the 'War of Jenkins's Ear', so Dr. Williams's highly influential book seems itself to have been partly a response to 'the Nootka Incident'.

Nootka Sound is an inlet on the western coast of Vancouver Island in Canada. The area was in dispute between Britain and Spain, since it had originally been visited by Juan Perez in 1774, and then by Captain Cook in 1778. Spain claimed the right at the time to the whole of the north-western coast of America, but the British argument was that a country could not own an area without occupying it. In 1789 the Spanish seized four British trading ships in Nootka Sound, thus threatening imminent war. This was averted (or at least postponed) by the Nootka Sound Convention, of 28th October 1790, by which Spain gave up the claim to a monopoly of trade and settlement in North America, evidently recognising Britain's superior strength and the likelihood of our attracting Prussian backing. This crucial achievement opened up the possibility of British settlement on the Pacific coast, and it coincides with one other remarkable event in London which brought the whole business of Britain's prior right to the Americas to the boil, ready indeed for the arrival of John Evans.

William Augustus Bowles was an Irish-American married to a Cherokee, had to a large extent gone native, and came to London in 1791, that crucial year, announcing himself as both 'General' Bowles, and as an Indian chief. He actually held some official position in relation to the Creek nation, but it was his flare for the romantic and flamboyant that made him such a success in George III's London. He wore either wild west leather hunting clothes or a brightly coloured turban with an ostrich feather, according apparently to his mood. He was strikingly good looking, and could hardly have been ignored. Nobility and royalty took him up. Tapping into the predominant interests of that year, and to a large extent himself stimulating them, Bowles amply confirmed the stories of the Welsh Indians. This came as a welcome gift to the 'Gwyneddigion Society', a cultural group formed among the London Welsh, which at this time was about to follow William Jones's suggestion and raise funds to send a suitable person (initially intended to be Iolo Morganwg) to America to find the Welsh Indians and of course convert them to Welsh Non-Conformism.

Yes, there were Welsh-speaking Indians, confirmed Bowles. He had it from a Welshman who had been with him who had conversed with them. They were called the Padoucas. The name, it was speculated at the time, was a corruption of 'Madogwys', the people of Madog. Actually it was the French term for the Commanches. He placed them somewhat vaguely to the west of the Mississippi, with enough references to get people looking carefully at maps. The expedition to communicate with the Padoucas was firmly forming in the minds of the Gwyneddigions when John Evans arrived.

That Iolo Morganwg would be the chosen person to go in search of them must have seemed obvious. Then aged 44, Edward Williams is one of the most colourful characters in the history of Welsh scholarship and the main promoter of the Welsh revival among the expatriate community in London. The Honourable Society of the Cymmrodorion had been founded in 1751, and the Gwyneddigion Society in 1770, laying the foundations of the formalisation of the London-Welsh. Iolo Morganwg (as he is always known, by his bardic name) came from Glamorgan, where he practised as a stonemason, and had moved to London in the 1770's, where he took part in meetings of the Welsh groups. Iolo was a knowledgeable scholar and a fervent collector of manuscripts. Unfortunately for Welsh antiquarianism it turned out much later that he had doctored and added to these in the cause of promoting his own beliefs about the purity of the descent of Welsh lore and culture from druidic times. It is then at least possible that the evidence of the Madocians survival in America which then inspired Dr. John Williams to bring out a second book (entitled *Further Observations on the Discovery of America...*, etc.) was given some assistance by Iolo's fruitful imagination. His own beliefs on the subject are quite clear. In his published English poetry, *Poems, Lyric and Pastoral*, of 1794, there is a long one about Madog's voyage:

Boast, CAMBRIA, boast thy sceptred Lord –
'Twas HE, thy MADOC, first explor'd,
   What bounds the Atlantic tide;
He, from the tumults of a Crown,
Sought shelter in a *world unknown*.
   With Heav'n his only guide.

The poem goes on to deal with the Madocians, and the desire to find them, so may perhaps have been written while Iolo still intended to be a main part of that enterprise:

We heard of late astonish'd Fame
Declare that still our MADOC'S name

Bids Glory's trump resound,
Where still, amid the desert wild,
A free-born race, of manners mild,
    Old *British* tribes are found.

I thither fly with anxious haste,
Will brave all dangers of the waste,
    Range tangled woods about;
Pierce ev'ry corner, like the wind,
Till Death forbids, or surely find
    My long-lost brethren out.

Iolo was a friend of Robert Southey, who later became Poet
Laureate, and it may be this work which originally inspired
Southey's long poem *Madoc*, published in 1805, where indeed
Iolo gets a mention:

Iolo, old Iolo, he who knows
The virtue of all herbs of mount or vale,
Or greenwood shade, or quiet brooklet's bed;
Whatever lore of science, or of song,
Sages and Bards of old have handed down.

By the beginning of 1792 the plans for Iolo's journey had
become elaborate. After toying with the idea of a southern
route, to reach the southernmost groups of Padoucas in
Arkansas, by March he had decided instead to go to
Philadelphia that August, and make his way via the Ohio to the
Missouri. He busied himself with establishing contacts and
introductions.

It was felt among the supporters of the expedition that Iolo
should not be allowed to go on this epic journey alone, and as
early as May 1792 he mentioned in correspondence "a young
man from Caernarvonshire" as a suitable companion. It seems,
then, that John Evans had by then arrived in London, perhaps

with a letter of introduction to the Gwyneddigion Society from Dafydd Ddu.

There are two tantalising puzzles lying at the root of the next event. Why did John Evans move to London, and why did Iolo drop out of the American expedition?

It is normally assumed that Evans went to London, like many other young men from North Wales of his time, indeed of any time, to seek his fortune. Although this is often described as 'going to London to live', he cannot have been there more than a few months when the plans started to take shape for him to leave again. Gwyn Williams says that while we do not know when he left Waunfawr, it seems likely to have been after June 1791, when Dafydd Ddu read his ode and William Jones published his address, although he could of course have been influenced by both these literary events in London. It may of course always have been his intention to take part in the American trip, inspired by the events of the 1791 eisteddfod, and all we really know is that John Evans was a person of quite remarkable impetuosity.

As to why Iolo pulled out, it is sometimes said that he was in financial difficulty, but so of course was Evans, and this failed to put him off. The expedition was not, in the end, funded, since the Gwyneddigion had decided to ask for government help, which would have been less likely to be procured if they had been fund-raising themselves. In the end John Evans was lent £20 for his passage, and travelled steerage, and this seems to have been all the money he had.

A likely explanation for Iolo's inability to go is his state of health, mental as well as physical. For most of his life he had been addicted to laudanum, a derivative of opium, and it was probably this condition which threw him at times into deep depression. The summer of 1792 seems to have been one of those times. He told his wife that for two weeks he had been unable to speak, a shock for such an apparently loquacious man. His mental state seems to have been paranoid at the least, possibly schizophrenic. It was perhaps just as well that Evans went instead.

He sailed in the late summer of 1792, perhaps from Liverpool, and arrived in Baltimore on 10th October. Welsh Methodism is a powerful network, in which John Evans was well-connected. As well as a letter from Iolo Morganwg to a Philadelphia book-seller, he had secured an introduction from the Rev. Thomas Charles of Bala (who became the founder of the Bible Society and the Sunday School Movement) to the Rev. Lewis Richards, a Welsh Baptist, in Baltimore. The latter gave him accommodation and in turn passed him on by way of a letter of introduction to the Rev. Samuel Jones in Philadelphia. Dr. Jones was a man of Glamorgan who had been in America since he was a child, was educated in Philadelphia and became minister of the Pennepek Baptist Church near Philadelphia in 1762. He was regarded by Welsh religious leaders as the main representative of the Welsh in America at this time.

Almost at once Evans was on his way north to visit Jones, who did not encourage him in his quest but warned him, instead, of the dangers of it. He returned to Baltimore for the winter, since there was no hope of setting out until the spring, got a job as a clerk in a merchant's counting house and started to learn surveying. In November, upon arrival, he had written at once to Iolo Morganwg. "You know that every Welshman is possessed of intrepidity of mind. It would have been easier with your humble servant had he been born without this quality, but as the Almighty saw it good to endow me with it, I will manage it to the glory of his Name! Is there one thing in the possession of Ieuan ab Ivan that he would not sacrifice to the cause of the Madogion? No, not one; even my precious life would I lay down for their sake." From Baltimore again he wrote to his brother in Waunfawr, on 'St Stephen's Day' (26th December), 1792.

The letter is significant for us because of what it tells us about John Evans. He tells his brother of his visit to the Rev. Samuel Jones, stretching the hundred mile journey from

Baltimore to Philadelphia to three hundred, and calling Dr. Jones, falsely, an American Senator. This gentleman, he said, had offered him a company of twenty armed men, 'for my security against the Indians'. He is somewhat star-struck by the wealth of the New World. The poor here live better than farmers in Wales, he says, and were his brother to sell the smallholding Tai'r Ffynnon, the money, here, would buy a property larger than Glynllifon. When we come to consider Evans's later evidence, we must bear these boastful exaggerations carefully in mind.

Some slight disappointment shows through the bombast of the December letter. Far from offering him an armed escort, Samuel Jones had actively discouraged him from his enterprise, as a result of which he was now back in Baltimore trying to earn enough money to go without further financial help. He tells his brother he is earning £50 (over how long?) and is among friends, though it seems that the Welsh community is not as Welsh or as extensive as he would have wished: to keep up his Welsh he talks to himself and sings whenever possible in the old language. He asks his brother to tell his friend – 'Dywed wrth fy nghar' – Dafydd Thomas, that is Dafydd Ddu Eryri, his old mentor, that he sang a carol by him, on Christmas Day.

In March next year he returned to Philadelphia, but once again was warned by his contacts there not to venture into Indian territory. Without their help or encouragement he then set off, across the Susquenhanna river and the Alleghanny Mountains to the Ohio river, which he travelled down for two weeks and seven hundred miles until it met the Mississippi. A river boat then took him a further two hundred miles up the Mississippi as far as its junction with the Missouri at St. Louis. The international territorial position in America at the time was complicated: the thirteen British colonies in the east had recently become America, and to the north the British were in occupation of Hudson Bay; the French held much of Canada and the Great Lakes, and they also controlled the area down the

Mississippi to New Orleans. It was the French who had founded St. Louis, and indeed when John Evans arrived it was still a French-speaking town. But the Spanish had in the meantime moved north from Mexico, and by international agreement both the French and the British gave up to Spain the rights over territory west of the Mississippi, which included St. Louis.

St. Louis was then quite a small town. It was home to about a thousand white people, mostly French, and some three hundred Negro slaves. The Governor at the time was Don Zenon Trudeau, and it fell to him to decide what to do about Evans. He assumed that he was an English agent, and put him in jail. Evidently the story that he was in search of Welsh-speaking Indians carried little weight. This, at any rate, is the itinerary normally given, for instance in Ellen Pugh's *Brave His Soul* and the source that apparently follows, David Williams's *John Evans and the Legend of Madoc*, both of which works have him in jail in St. Louis for nearly two years. This is because they have missed out an earlier attempt to go up the Missouri, being in their turn misled by the edited summary of Evans's later letter to Dr. Samuel Jones, describing his travels, which had appeared in the press after being more or less re-written by Morgan John Rhys, a propagandist for Welsh freedom, the founder of *Y Cylchgrawn Cymmraeg*, a magazine which closely followed Evans's adventures. As it happens the letter in which Evans himself describes his travels survives, in the Mrs. Irving H. McKesson collection kept by the Historical Society of Pennsylvania, and it is published by Gwyn Williams as an appendix to his paper *John Evans's Mission to the Madogwys, 1792-1799*, in The Bulletin of the Board of Celtic Studies in 1978.

According to this he went first to Fort Pitt, where he waited for a month for high waters. In a few days then he got to Limestone in Kentucky, then travelled by land as far as 'Cincinata', where he stayed a few days before moving on, evidently by boat, into Louisiana. There he encountered the political situation for the first time, being 'obliged to take the

Oath of Allegiance before I could be permitted to debark.' This evidently posed no problem for him. He then (at New Madrid, on the Mississippi) fell ill with a fever. He was well looked after by the Welsh contacts he had, a pattern which runs through his American adventures. If we are to believe him he had set out from Philadelphia with a dollar and three quarters in his pocket.

The fever abated after two months. While still not fully recovered he decided to press on, with one man for company (he does not say who). It seems from his account a hopelessly unplanned trip, since neither of them knew the way and they at once got lost. It is hard to understand that though the plan was to travel up the Missouri they were walking through wilderness with no apparent sight of the river. Still feverish, he waded though swamps for miles, and after a week reached a Spanish post in Illinois. Some of the detail reads rather as a traveller's extravagant tale: he walked for miles "in water from the hip to the Arm Pitt amongst a numerous crowd of the bigest water reptiles I ever saw". The implication is that these were alligators, in which case Evans would certainly not have survived this paddle. But if they were not, and if they indeed existed, what could they possibly be, and why is he not more specific on the subject?

He stayed then with another Welshman on the American side of the Mississippi. Remarkably he says he stayed there two years waiting for a chance to travel up the Missouri, where the Spanish and the Indians posed problems. He then heard of 'a gent. at St. Louis who was engaged to go up the aforesaid River'. This, we know, was James Mackay, a Scotsman working for the Spanish, who had already been told about John Evans and his search for the Welsh Indians, having, in this unexpectedly small world, met Morgan John Rhys in Cincinnati, where the latter was planning to found a Welsh colony.

Mackay had been charged by the Spanish with undertaking an expedition for the Missouri Company, to find a route from the upper Missouri across the Rockies to the other Spanish colony on the Pacific. Mackay had visited the Mandans in 1787, then working for the French North-West Company, and he knew them to be crucial to the enterprise. Since John Evans was also in effect on a mission to the Mandans it was hardly surprising that in the end they would get together.

Two previous expeditions had failed, beset by hostile Indians. British contact from Canada had, it was thought, reached the Mandans, and threatened the Spanish enterprise. Evans crossed the river into St. Louis specifically to find Mackay, thinking that it was, as he says, 'now or never'. He realised at the same time that 'it was rather a ridiculous busyness as it was a Critical time on Spanish side', and sure enough he was at once 'taken for a Spy, Imprisoned, loaded with iron and put in the Stoks. Here I suffered very much for several days till my friends from the American side came and proved to the Contrary and I was released.' Prone as he seems to have been to exaggeration, he would not have described two years as several days, so that we must see his incarceration as being short.

He set out with Mackay in August, the expedition now rather precariously financed since in the wake of the previous two disasters half the shareholders of the Missouri Company had resigned. A colourful adventurer, Jacques Clamorgan, who had come from the West Indies via Canada to St. Louis, seems to have been the motive force behind the enterprise, with the backing of the Governor of Louisiana. Clamorgan, sometimes known as Clan-Morgan, seems himself to have been Welsh by background, and maybe thus had an interest in finding the Mandans.

They had about thirty men with them, travelling with four large dug-out canoes which carried gifts for the Indians and supplies to last the two years the trip was expected to take. They went up the Missouri from St. Louis, and after six weeks reached the Platte river, at Omaha, in Nebraska. They overwintered with the Omaha Indians, and Mackay built a fort which he named Fort Charles, near to where Sioux City stands today. Evans went hunting buffalo with the Indians on a twenty-five day trip, a remarkable feat for a white man in the middle of winter. They waited then for the Missouri to unfreeze.

In the meantime Mackay was involved in arranging a conference of Indian chiefs, with the help of the powerful Omaha chief Black Bird, with the aim of negotiating trade agreements on behalf of the Spanish crown, presumably before the British could get there. Reports had reached him that the French Canadians had set up a British post for the North-West Company at the 'great bend' of the Missouri, having reached the Mandans there from Lake Winnipeg. Rather than jeopardise his plans for an Indian assembly by leaving at this point, he sent John Evans on with a small party in early February 1796. After travelling 300 miles overland (since the river was still frozen) Evans encountered the hostile Sioux and was obliged to hasten back to Fort Charles.

When he went again in June Evans was more fortunate. Travelling by boat now, but slowly up the fast-flowing river, he carefully mapped the country as he crossed it, the first to have charted the river and its tributaries. Seven hundred miles up from Fort Charles he came to the Arikara Indians in early August. This led to a six week delay while they continued to demand his goods. Somehow he persuaded them to let him go, and on 23rd September he reached the first Mandan village.

Within five days then he had turned the British fur traders (who now controlled the previously French North-West Company) out of the fort they had built, renaming it Fort Mackay. In an act of fierce irony he ran down the Union Flag and raised the flag of Spain. We were, as it happened, though he could not have known this, two weeks away from declaring war on Spain, so that this is normally regarded as an act of treason. It is remarked in a leaflet provided by the Antur Waenfawr that this act may have had further international implications: it 'may have had some bearing on the fact that North Dakota is today in U.S. Territory and not Canadian'.

Evans got on well with the Mandans, staying with them then during the bitter northern winter. He studied their ways and customs, and in the course of that winter evidently came to his much-cited conclusion, which he wrote to Dr. Samuel Jones, in his letter from St. Louis on his return, dated 15th July, 1797.

> Thus having explored and charted the Missurie for 1800 miles and by my Communications with the Indians this side of the Pacific Ocean from 35 to 49 Degrees of Latitude, I am able to inform you that there is no such People as the Welsh Indians, and you will be so kind as to satisfie my Friends as to that doubtfull Question.

Reaction to this paragraph, when it was reported back in Wales, took several forms. It was thought by some that Evans had simply not gone far enough. It was known that the Welsh Indians lived much further up the Missouri than he had been. It is also clear, of course, that the fact that John Evans had not found them cannot be taken to prove that they did not exist. The most obvious reason for casting doubt on the reliability of his statement is that he was working for the Crown of Spain. The story of the Welsh Indians had always been a piece of anti-Spanish propaganda. Indeed the Spanish were aware of this themselves. In 1797, that same year, the Governor of Louisiana had issued the explicit instruction: "It is in the interest of his Catholic Majesty that the reports of British Indians in Mandan country be denied once and for all.." At least this is as quoted by Gwyn Williams in his 1978 paper, where he says in a footnote that he had 'not yet laid hold of this publication, but it is certainly authentic'. If so, then it would in itself be sufficient to show that even if John Evans had in fact discovered Welsh Indians he could not have said so. In fact the coda 'you will be so kind as to satisfie my friends as to that doubtfull Question' is consistent with a mission to destroy the story.

The significant words of Gayoso had previously been quoted by Ellen Pugh, whose footnote says the relevant papers are in the Spanish archives in Seville. Pugh in fact sees more in this than Williams. The fact that it was this same Governor, Gayoso de Lemos, who took Evans into his care in the end seems to her to prove that `he had been lying under orders. It was a precaution against his speaking out, in his delirium or in his cups. There is a hearsay anecdote – 'the written memorandum of an acquaintance' - which Pugh appears to have got from Deacon, whose sources are hard to trace, that Evans once did just that. "When heavily in strong liquor he bragged to his friends in St. Louis that the Welsh Indians would keep their secret to their graves because he had been handsomely paid to keep quiet on the subject."

Running short of supplies, and so of gifts for the Indians, Evans found his position, along with his health, was weakening. He knew that he was nowhere near the Missouri's source, having measured the width of the river at that point as 1000 metres. He had neither the men nor the equipment to proceed. In March the Canadians, taking advantage of his situation, arrived with gifts and attempted to win back the support of the Mandans and have John Evans killed, and the fact that this failed is a tribute to the Mandans' affection for him. There was no future for him on the Missouri now, however, and in May they let him go. He promised to come back with arms and goods, but of course he never did.

Back at Fort Charles he found that Mackay had left and the Missouri Company was bankrupt. 'In July 1797 I arrived at St. Louis after the long voyage of 2 years up the Missurie, Was well received by the Officers of this Please...' That the transcript given in Gwyn Williams's appendix is accurate, with its wayward spelling and eccentric use of capitals, is shown by the good photograph of the original which may be seen in the John Evans room at the Antur Waenfawr.

He expected to go on another trip. Instead the Spanish employed him for a time as a land surveyor, mapping the lands allotted to the controlled immigrations from America. He settled for a time on the banks of the Mississippi. Failing health obliged him to give this up, and the Governor of New Orleans took him into his house. He had apparently exacerbated his illness by excessive drinking. He wrote an uncharacteristically angry note to Samuel Jones in November 1798, complaining about the publication of his Missouri letter in the American press. In May 1799 Gayoso, the Governor, wrote to Mackay: "Poor Evans is very ill; ... the strength of liquor has deranged his head; he has been out of his senses for several days…" A letter dated 3rd August 1799 from Daniel Clark in New Orleans to Dr. Samuel Jones in Philadelphia read: "The inclosed letter from you to Mr. John Evans fell lately into my hands and I was induced to open it, that by learning the residence of some of his friends I might advise them of the fate of that unfortunate man who died not long since in this City, after being for some time deprived of his reason. Chagrin and disappointment in his Views contributed, I fear, to hasten his end."

He died at the age of 29. Since the Governor himself is said to have died of Yellow Fever it was possibly in the course of a Yellow Fever epidemic, so that might have been the cause. Tuberculosis however ran in his family, and it is also speculated that his suffering during the severe winter he spent with the Mandans might have brought this on.

Although his mission itself, to find the Welsh Indians and convert them to Methodism, apparently failed, the work John Evans did on the Missouri in the end contributed to history. President Thomas Jefferson had two copies of Evans's maps in his possession when, in 1803, he made the Louisiana Purchase.

Jefferson's family originated in Llanberis, in North Wales, and he had never lost sight of his roots. By the great good fortune of the Louisiana purchase he doubled the territory held by the American states, acquiring for 15 million dollars all the country between Canada and the Gulf of Mexico bordered by the Rocky Mountains and the Mississippi. Evans's maps gave him some idea of the form of this, and he commissioned the explorers Meriwether Lewis and William Clark to investigate it further, giving them copies of Evans's maps. Hearing the provenance of the maps – that Evans had been looking for Welsh Indians - Jefferson told Lewis and Clark to keep their eyes open for the Madogwys on the Missouri. The two adventurers did in fact reach the Mandans, and, ten years after Evans, proceeded to find the long-sought route from the upper Missouri across to the Pacific; but they did not report on the Mandans, or anyone else, speaking Welsh.

One of the maps of this expedition, originally attributed to Clark, has subsequently been identified as a copy of one of Evans's maps. It is now in the Beinecke Rare Books Library at Yale University. Many of Evans's papers went back from New Orleans to Spain, and are lodged in the Archive of the 'Indias' in Seville. A map by Clark which incorporates the information from Evans and Mackay is in the Library of Congress at Washington.

Much has been made of Evans's crucial statement by those who wish to impose on the story of Madog their final refutation. Quite without doubt the most meticulous and best-researched, the most decisively conclusive investigation of this whole frustrating and absorbing matter, is that written by Thomas Stephens in 1858, later published (posthumously) by Longmans in 1893.

Stephens ran a chemist shop in Merthyr Tydfil and as a scholar he was largely self-taught. He had been winning prizes at the eisteddfodau around Wales since the 1840's, and published an important book *The Literature of the Kymry* in 1849. There was a prize offered at the Llangollen eisteddfod in September 1858 'For the best essay upon the discovery of America in the twelfth century by Prince Madoc ab Owain Gwynedd'. It was £20 and a silver star. Stephens went in for it.

All works on the subject subsequent to this have, directly or at second or third hand, been indebted to the result, including of course this one. So comprehensive and well structured is Stephens's 'essay' that (as has often been remarked) no more books would seem to be necessary on the subject – yet very many have been written since, leaving us with the conclusion that the matter simply will not go away. In thus setting out to kill the Madog story off – "It is to be hoped that my countrymen may henceforth feel that they degrade themselves, and heap discredit upon our motherland, by giving evidence to this idle and unfounded tale" – Stephens in fact leaves us with the ultimate question, as to why it will not die.

Ironically he did not win the competition. There were six entries, the other five affirming the story. The committee considered Stephens's to be not on the given subject, so excluded it: a treatise "on the non-discovery of America ought not be received, there being no such subject in the programme". There was a big row over this, and indeed one suspects foul play. The judges resented interference from the committee. One resigned. Another, the Rev. D. Sylvan Evans, a lexicographer, wrote to the secretaries of the committee that Thomas Stephens was "by far the ablest writer" and since the other entries "fall far short of establishing the points which their respective writers have undertaken to prove" he refused to judge between them. This letter was suppressed, but no award was given. At what would have been the award ceremony Thomas Stephens himself appeared, stepped on the platform and claimed permission to say a few words. This was resisted by the Chairman, but he was obliged to give way to audience demand. Stephens defended his work ably. The eisteddfod should above all promote the truth and not support claims which could not be proved. It turned out that one of the other entries was by one of the secretaries of the committee which had ruled him out.

His work is painstakingly thorough. He starts with the literary sources and historical testimonies, though he could not have known, of course, of the doubt later to be cast on any work which had been in the library of Iolo Morganwg. He then moves on to the 'travellers' tales', listing twelve people reported indirectly to have encountered Welsh Indians, and eight who themselves reported having spoken Welsh to them. How, one wonders, can his avowed scepticism counter such a weight of evidence? It turns out that he considers all these to be variants of the original tale by Morgan Jones.

It is, in any case, he says, the sheer abundance of the evidence which undermines it. It "lacks definiteness and consistency; so that, after all, there has been much uncertainty as to who the Welsh Indians really were…" They were too widely spread to have been factual. "Thus pretty nearly the whole of America, from Canada to Cuba, or even Peru, has been at various times claimed as the local habitation of the Madogwys: they have been found, generally speaking, everywhere on the new continent…" Everywhere, he concludes, has proved to be another form of nowhere.

Stephens's demand for rigorous scholarship occasionally goes against him, as when for instance he criticises one writer for "being so careless as to place the death of John Evans at New Orleans", thinking he died at St. Louis – whereas we know from the letter of August 1799 to Samuel Jones that Evans died in New Orleans. He can be archly amusing, as when, writing about himself from the anonymity of the eisteddfod competition (which he entered under the bardic pseudonym of Gwrnerth Ergydlym) he calls himself "a self-educated Welsh druggist at Merthyr Tydfil", of whom, he says, … "it is evident that he had not finally made up his mind on the subject" when writing the *Literature of the Kymry*, but in an essay in 1856 his views seem to have hardened: "It is, therefore, manifest that, whatever value may be attached to the judgements of Mr. Stephens, the Madoc narrative has been weighed in his balance and found wanting."

In the end, on the question of 'Are there Welsh Indians?' Stephens probably quite rightly sees the two essential witnesses as Morgan Jones and John Evans. Since it seems that he did not know of the existence of the letter from St. Louis, but only of reports of what Evans said in a magazine called Greal in 1800, he quotes from this: "With reference to the Welsh Indians, he says that he was unable to meet with any such people; and he has come to the fixed conclusion, which he has founded upon his acquaintance with various tribes, *that there are no such people in existence.*" We for our part know this to be an accurate report; but for Stephens it is unsourced and at best second hand, and for him to rely on it entirely, while constantly casting doubt on other evidence, is a blemish on his scholarship. Moreover as far as he could see Evans came to his conclusion only through his "acquaintance with various tribes" rather than as a result of any exhaustive search. Since Stephens did not, from this report, know exactly what Evans said, and under what circumstances, it is surprising that he puts so much reliance on it. We know too, which perhaps he did not, that John Evans was not always accurate (or it might be said truthful) in his statements.

Rather more convincingly Stephens points out that Lewis and Clark "had special instructions to look out for the Welsh Indians", reached the Mandans in November 1804 and stayed with them until April 05, and he concludes that "if there had been Welsh Indians on the Missouri, they would have been found by Lewis and Clark".

Morgan Jones poses him a problem. He faces up to the fact that Morgan Jones was a most unlikely person to lie, and deftly twists it to his own purpose: "if he, a minister of the Gospel, and a man having the advantages of an Oxford education, could either have been grossly self-deceived or have been so wilfully deceitful towards others, what other testimony can have any claim to acceptance?" He admits that Morgan Jones "was qualified to judge as to what was or was not Welsh; and his statement must necessarily be either strictly true or manifestly false, for it cannot be placed on any intermediate ground". He finds the internal evidence of Jones's letter unsatisfactory. Jones, he says, confuses three expeditions, and shows a weak grasp of the history, the people and the location of Indian tribes of the period. He concludes that he was not recounting his own experiences, but had "some indistinct knowledge" and "a hearsay knowledge of these events". But of course he ignores the fact that Morgan Jones was recalling an experience which took place some twenty-five years earlier, and any inaccuracies might be simply flaws of memory. In any case Thomas Stephens, who had presumably never been to America, is here placing himself as a superior authority on the early location of American Indian tribes to someone who had actually lived there at the time. His strongest argument against the veracity of the Jones story is that Jones, who must certainly have known of Madog, does not refer to the legend. His affecting not to be referring to Madog when announcing the discovery of Welsh-speaking Indians certainly casts the greatest doubt on his sincerity.

In the end Stephens concludes, and we may conclude with him, that John Evans and Morgan Jones are the two ultimate first-hand authorities, the one negative and the other affirmative. On the face of it Stephens has a problem justifying his particular use of these witnesses, arguing, as he must to suit his case, that John Evans's evidence is conclusive, Morgan Jones's in doubt. After all Evans is in the impossible position of claiming to prove a negative. He has come to the conclusion that there are no such people as Welsh-speaking Indians, but on any logical basis his reasoning (that there must be none, because he has not found them) is flawed.

Morgan Jones, on the other hand, said he had spoken Welsh with Indians, and Thomas Stephens admits that he cannot possibly have been mistaken as to what is or is not Welsh. He thus has to suppose that Morgan Jones was lying, whereas John Evans was telling the truth. In the end, as with all detective work, there is the overriding matter of motive. If we wished to doubt Evans's veracity, we need look no further than his circumstances. He was in the pay of the Spanish Crown. It would have been extremely foolish of him to have announced the discovery of Welsh Indians.

With Morgan Jones, however, this question of motive is a major problem. What could possibly have induced the man of God so explicitly and formally to lie? Stephens explains the story as possibly "intended as a hoax", and at the same time as an echo of the adventures, in 1604, of Captain John Smith, who was captured by the Indians. Of this he says quite inaccurately "We have here all the prominent features of Jones's narrative", whereas in fact we have none of them, but a different set altogether. The essence of the Jones story is the conversing in Welsh, and this of course is unique to it at the time. Certainly the story is fundamentally hard to swallow, but our inability to believe it does not, in the academic terms in which Stephens is dealing, constitute proof that it is false.

Stephens devotes some time to Indian languages, displaying a remarkable apparent knowledge of their grammar and vocabulary. In the process he tries to discredit George Catlin, whom he admits is the Madogwys' strongest ally, "the most respectable witness that has yet appeared on their behalf". He does not have much time for Catlin's linguistic tables: "…it must be evident, to anyone who examines these columns with a critical eye, that the writer had only a very imperfect acquaintance with the Welsh language…", which is probably true. Indian languages, he says (though on what basis?) bear some relation to all Asiatic and European tongues, not just Welsh. "and the Mandan canoe, as figured by Catlin, has no resemblance to the Welsh coracle." Is this a subjective judgement? Stephens does not specify in what respects it varies, whereas the skin and framework form is clearly held in common by the two. He rehearses Catlin's points: the Mandans are different; they have coracles; their language he thinks is like Welsh; they are a mixture of civilised and savage. These are dismissed with an arbitrary judgement which Stephens makes no attempt to substantiate: "These are all arguments that assume the point to be proved, and it is evident that Mr. Catlin shines more as a pictorial than as a critical writer."

In the end his show of scholarship and profession of objectivity do not entirely stand up to scrutiny. When he presents the evidence, in the early chapters, we cannot help noticing that he does not, as he claims, lay it before us just as it is, but adds his own decidedly partial comments. When setting before us, in a later chapter, 'The Affirmative' case, he shows it repeatedly in an unfavourable light. Rather surprisingly, when dealing with the historical Madog and finding that the Chronicles do not record his voyage, he does not consider that this might be because the prince never existed, so that they do not, in fact, mention him at all. It is indeed surprising, in view of his mission to destroy the story, that he accepts without question the supposition that Madog existed, and in fact has him dying in battle, never having left his own country. He does not spot the bard Cynddelw's ambiguity in the use of the word 'teulu', which we mentioned in Chapter Two, taking it to mean Madog the son of Owain, rather than, as seems likely, the companion. Based on this misunderstanding he has Madog dying 'two years at least' before his supposed voyage.

Did this possibility of his non-existence somehow not suit his purpose? Would the essay, perhaps, not have been achievable without its protagonist – Hamlet without the Prince? Or did he simply not think of this possibility at all – and if the last of these hypotheses, can we still believe in his reputation for incisive intellect, which we have already had occasional reason to doubt? Should we, then, perhaps put the origins of that reputation down to his remarkably lucid prose-style?

Once you have admitted that possibility, the famous 'essay' can be seen in a different light. Far from objective and impartial, it is a clever piece of advocacy. The work resembles a sermon, in character, rather than a lecture, seeking as it does rather to convert than to inform.

sevenseven

stones and stories

It is a long way from Mobile Bay to the home of the Mandan Indians, near Bismarck, on the bend of the Missouri. If it is to be supposed that Madog landed in Alabama and that the Mandans were the remnant of his people, folktale has to get the Madogwys from the one place to the other. Certainly George Catlin was able to argue convincingly, from signs of their former habitations, that the Mandans had moved up from the Ohio. Yet he too was anxious, at that point, to link them to the supposed Welsh colony. There is, on the face of it, no particular reason for the Mobile Bay landing, in the first place, except tradition. It is sometimes mentioned (for instance by Ellen Pugh and Richard Deacon) that in 1519 a Portuguese map-maker, Diego Ribeiro, working for the Spanish, drew a line pointing to Mobile Bay on which he wrote the words 'Tierra de los Gales', Land of the Welsh. The map is now in a cartographical collection in Seville, and the wording is not otherwise explained. Mobile Bay is, of course, a natural place to land. Currents naturally carry the seafarer coming down the coast into the Gulf of Mexico, and various early explorers, including Amerigo Vespucci, had ended up there.

Much work has been done to fill in the movement northwards, and Catlin himself mentions 'those numerous *civilised* fortifications, the ruins of which are now to be seen on the Ohio and the Muskingum' as being the work of the migrating Welsh. The first clear reference to these ruins in this connection comes in a letter of October 1810 from the Governor of Tennessee John Sevier, answering a question about the Welsh Indians. Nearly thirty years earlier Sevier had been fighting the Cherokee in the Tennessee valley, when "during the route I had discovered traces of very ancient, though regular fortifications".

He asked an old chief about these, presumably after having first made peace. Oconostota had been by then the ruling chief of the Cherokee nation for nearly sixty years so that if Sevier reports him truly his information is of unusual value.

"The old Chief immediately informed me: 'It is handed down by the Forefathers that the works had been made by White people who had formerly inhabited the country now called Carolina.'" They had been ousted eventually by the Cherokee and moved up the Missouri. "I then asked him if he had ever heard any of his ancestors saying what nation of people these Whites belonged to. He answered he 'had heard his grandfather and father say they were a people called Welsh, and that they had crossed the Great Water and landed first near the mouth of the Alabama River near Mobile...'" It is, we feel, almost as if Oconostota was recalling something told to his ancestors by John Evans.

In the 19th century there were five forts known of in the Chattanooga area "which" (according to Judge John Haywood in his History of Tennessee, of 1823) "had been built by white people living there before the Indian occupation". Now we can only clearly identify three, and these are mostly in a poor state of preservation and not well presented.

Lookout Mountain lies near the junction of the Alabama and Coosa rivers, forty-three miles south of Chattanooga. It is a place best known for the picturesque De Soto falls, near which, as described in 1833, the remains of fortifications could be seen, including a number of small rooms with constricted entrances. Now the remains have been much robbed and (according to Deacon) "all that is left is a hump covered by the mould of dead leaves", and to Pugh, revealing her source, "all that remains is a mound covered over with dead leaves".

It is rather surprising, in view of the poor state of the remains, that a surveyor from Kentucky discovered that the plan of this fort was "nearly identical" (to quote Pugh) "in layout and placement, to Dolwyddelan Castle in Gwynedd, the supposed birthplace of Madog." This is a mistake based on a confusion of dates. Dolwyddelan Castle has been much altered, and in its present romantic form belongs largely to the late 1840's. It is unlikely even that Llywelyn the Great, who would have been Madog's nephew, could have been born there, since the earliest parts of the structure seem to belong to the first decades of the 13th century, too late for Llywelyn's birth in the 1170's, and far too late for Madog's. An older castle indeed stood on a hillock across the road, but it seems as if this is not the one which the Kentucky surveyor measured.

A little better preserved is the rampart on Fort Mountain, a peak in the Cohutta Range in Georgia, 70 miles east of Chattanooga, a long protective stone wall built, as is the style with Welsh hillforts, on the only accessible slope of the hill. Ellen Pugh quotes Hughes Reynolds, author of *Coosa River Valley*, as saying that this wall "was built with the skill of military engineers with such angles that all parts of the wall could be defended. Such a defensive work was fully up to the standards of early European military science and far beyond the ability of the Indians to construct unaided". The Indians apparently built forts constructed out of palisades, not with stone walls.

Fort Mountain is now a State Park of the state of Georgia, and so is well interpreted and protected. The local 'Sherpa' guide says of the fort "Archeologists and historians have been unable to solve the puzzle of who, if anyone, built the wall or why or when they built it. There are many theories. A favorite explanation is that the wall was built by the Woodland Indians around 500 a.d." The writers see it as some sort of ceremonial centre, rather than a defensive work. "The east-west orientation of its end points would result in alignment at sunrise and sunset at the solar equinox in both spring and fall." They comment on its dramatic setting and extensive views, which "could have added to its religious significance. Ceremonial centers similar to this one were built by the Woodland Indians at Old Stone Fort,

Tennessee, and Rock Eagle Mound in Putnam County, Georgia. The Woodland Indians occupied the Southeast from several centuries b.c. to about 900 a.d." There is thus no need to posit a Welsh invasion, since American history is very much longer than many people (including many Americans) realise.

The Sherpa Guide does not, however, quite forget Madog. "A less probable but more romantic theory attributes the wall to a legendary Welsh prince named Medoc (sic). He supposedly sailed into Mobile, Alabama, 500 years ago, then worked his way northward toward the Fort Mountain vicinity. Nothing else is known about Prince Medoc, except that his name is vaguely linked to several petroglyphs found in other parts of the Southeast."

The best example of the mysterious stone forts and perhaps the most famous is the Old Stone Fort at Manchester, Tennessee, on the Duck River, 70 miles west of Chattanooga.

"One theory," says the notice on the approach, as to the Fort's provenance, "is that it was built by a party of 12th Century Welsh voyagers who entered the country via the Gulf of Mexico." It has long been known that this fort, and by extension the other similar ones, date from before Columbus. Judge John Haywood, who made a particular study of the antiquities of Tennessee in the 19th century, reports that a tree growing in the wall of the fort was cut down in 1819 and found to have 357 rings, which would take it back to 1462. It turns out that the fort itself (if that is what it is) is considerably older than that.

For once we know, and do not need to speculate, since the state purchased the surrounding area in 1966 and at once appointed the Department of Anthropology of the University of Tennessee to investigate. The results are published in a booklet by a member of the team, Charles H. Faulkner.

The anthropologists were concerned with three principal questions: Who built the structure? When? And what was it for? They came up with conclusive answers to the first of these, but the third is still debated. The enclosure was constructed by Middle Woodland Indians, "known to have lived in Tennessee shortly after the birth of Christ", the first users of agriculture in the Southeast, whose villages may be found in the land around within twenty miles of the enclosure, the largest being about three miles downstream. "There is little doubt," says Faulkner, "that a prehistoric group of American Indians built the enclosure known as the Old Stone Fort. Local legends giving Norsemen and the Welsh as builders are not based on fact, since there is no archaeological evidence of European migrants in the southeastern interior of this continent during the first four or five centuries of the Christian Era. A lack of contact between Europe and the Southeast at this time is almost universally accepted among professional archaeologists."

It cannot have been built by the followers of Madog, we thus find, because it was too old. Carbon dated samples gave the team dates from AD 30 to AD 430. In other words, if Madog and his people had come this way, in the last years of the 12th century, they would have found the Old Stone Fort already here – and already old. The Welshmen might well have recognised some of its features.

The enclosure is typical of such structures in having walls on the sides which are most easily ascended, and none above the virtual cliffs which rise over the Duck and Little Duck rivers, which meet at this point. It also has an apparently defensive entrance, a feature which is rare, shared only by another 'Old Fort' in Missouri. These features would certainly suggest defence as a function, but "whether the purpose of these structures was defense has been seriously questioned, especially by more recent authors". One of the reasons for doubting its defensive purpose is the virtual absence of debris within the site. "If the enclosures were built to be occupied in time of danger, some of them were apparently never needed." This is consistent with its being a ceremonial site, since such were kept clean. The walls are thus seen as preventing intrusion by the uninvited, the elaborate entrance as also excluding intruders and providing a setting for ceremonial entry.

Faulker lists nine examples of stone and earth walled enclosures in the Southeast, including those we have mentioned on Fort Mountain and at the De Soto Falls. They have revealed little or no cultural material, and are associated with the Middle Woodland Indians by the few dates they have revealed and the presence of those Indians in their neighbourhoods The standard guidebook, *The Tennessee Handbook*, is decisive on the issue:

> Speculation held that Hernando De Soto, roving Vikings, or some obscure Welsh prince built the fort. Under closer examination, however, these theories faded away. Studies by the University of Tennessee date the structure to the Indians of the Woodland period – about AD 30 – 430.

None of this deters Ellen Pugh. "Finally, after occupying each of these lesser defenses, the Welsh settlers moved on and built their final major bulwark – Old Stone Fort, on the Duck River…" Pugh then mentions the finding of three Roman coins 'well over a hundred years ago' during the excavation of a site for cellars 'near Old Stone Fort', two coins at Manchester, one at Fayetteville. A full description of one of them appeared in a Philadelphia newspaper, on August 22nd 1818, from which description it was judged much later by an American numismatist to have been "a denarius of Antonius Pius", by which I suppose is meant Antoninus Pius, which would put it at some date between 138 and 161 AD. Pugh speculates, with more than her usual wild abandon, that "it is entirely possible that Madog's twelfth-century colonists brought some of these already ancient coins with them", though why on earth they should do this she does not suggest.

These coins, which presumably at once disappeared (since their later whereabouts are not mentioned), making their improbable appearance in connection with the Old Stone Fort, turn up again on a plaque the existence of which itself is highly unlikely, but this time is well attested by photograph and witness. Its authorities for its claim about Madoc, it inscribes, include the Encyclopedia Americana 1918 edition, Webster's Encyclopedia, Hakluyt, Ridpath's History of the World, and "ancient Roman coins found in Forts in Tenn. These Forts," the inscription continues, "resemble the Forts of Wales of the 9th and 10th centuries and of the white Indians of the Tennessee and Missouri rivers".

According to my informant Jerry Yares, of Maryville, Tennessee, the plaque itself was last heard of in storage in the attic of the visitor centre at Fort Morgan, Mobile, where it was erected on 10th November 1953 by the Virginia Cavalier Chapter of the Daughters of the American Revolution. This is an often strange story, that of Madog, and few parts of it are stranger than the existence of this plaque. When Jerry Yares asked why it was in the attic the lady in charge replied that they had grown tired of replacing it when it kept getting stolen. He asked whom she suspected, and she replied 'Those Knights of Columbus people, I suppose!'

The plaque reads:

IN MEMORY OF PRINCE MADOC, A WELSH EXPLORER, WHO LANDED ON THE SHORES OF MOBILE BAY IN 1170 AND LEFT BEHIND, WITH THE INDIANS, THE WELSH LANGUAGE.

conclusion

So we have taken Madog all the way from the unlikely point of his departure in the quiet domestic garden of a house in Rhos-on-Sea to his unlikely point of arrival in the historic theme park at Fort Morgan. After following such a journey, and indeed passing beyond it up the Missouri, what are we to conclude?

In the course of writing this book I have indeed come to a number of conclusions, and I hope the book itself will show how this has happened.

Firstly, we get the story of Prince Madog ab Owain Gwynedd and his voyage largely from an attempt to discredit the justice of Spain's claim to the Americas, by right of primary discovery, at the height of the wars which culminated in the Spanish Armada. This was probably not a complete invention at the time, but based on a Welsh memory of a folk tradition of a seafarer called Madog; and it had a likely historical basis too in the memories of early voyages west.

The story later became embellished with false substantiation when it was used again for a similar purpose in subsequent Spanish wars.

It is practically certain that there was no such historical personage as this Prince Madog, son of Owain Gwynedd, though a confusion might have arisen from references in old Welsh literature to another Madog, who was a member of his warband (but was not said to have explored or found new countries). The answer to the primary question must then, reluctantly, be 'no'. Prince Madog did not discover America, because he did not exist.

Similarly one must answer no for another reason, that is that 'discover' is not the right verb, because there was no such event. America was entered by a gradual wave-movement of nomadic tribes, from Asia, perhaps the Pacific, and possibly even Europe, in late Ice-Age times. By the time Europeans became sufficiently conscious of the world to get round to making maps various flourishing and sophisticated cultures were already well established there. Moreover if the question implies the thought 'before Columbus', this fails to become affirmative as well, since it is certain that America's existence was known of in Europe before Christopher Columbus's time, even if he himself seems to have been ignorant of it, but it was the Vikings, rather than the Welsh, who first went there, long before the time of the supposed Madog.

The idea, absurd in itself, of Welsh-speaking, white-skinned Indians, so persistent and so plentifully attested since the time of the first immigrants, is, ironically, much harder to negate. In the end there is something not fully explained here. Why, if there were (as one instinctively supposes) no Welsh-speaking Indians, did so many people attest to having spoken with them in Welsh? The contrary evidence – which could show that they were lying, and so we would simply have to say why – is missing. I do not myself feel, however, that linguistic analysis shows conclusively that the Mandans – since it is they, in the end, who are left with this burden – spoke anything identifiable as being related to Welsh.

It is ironic too that the best display of evidence, in supposed dismissal of the matter, can be shown to be flawed. The two main witnesses brought forward rather spoil their own testimony, in that John Evans (for the prosecution) had good reason for lying, Morgan Jones (for the defence) however none. Our instincts incline us to believe the motivated liar, and disbelieve the most integrated witness; but this is subjective and partial, so hardly academic, so that we must leave the matter open.

Archaeological inquiry does not, either, lead us to an affirmative conclusion. There were Indians in pre-historic America capable of building stone forts which, like the Mandan coracles, and like much else, could have arrived at the same form as early Welsh ones from the need of the time and the circumstances and the opportunities and materials available. In any case it is now known that Indian culture was comparatively advanced long, long before the time of the Madocians, so that they would not need to be shown how to do anything by the Welsh.

There remains the one salient and unassailable fact: the legend of Madog is still persistent and compelling now, and will, all who write on the subject are convinced, continue indefinitely to be so. It has lasted now in healthy form for several hundred years, and I am sure that this book will not be the last word to be said on the subject. In the meantime the Prince Madog Society meets every third Tuesday at a pub in the Vale of Glamorgan, and groups in America and on the Internet continue to debate the matter and exchange ideas.

In that sense, and perhaps several others, the case for answering 'yes' to the question seems very powerful. Not perhaps Prince Madog, but some people for whom he stands, went to America at an early time, long before Columbus. If they were Welsh with Viking connections, which is not unlikely, then a son of Owain Gwynedd is a fit representative of them. There is no evidence for this, no evidence at all – except the persistence and the potency of the legend.

aknowledgements

The author wishes to thank the following for their assistance with his research:

Wil Aaron; David Atkinson; Mark Beardsall; Professor Bernard Knight; Gwen Manchester;

The management of Antur Waenfawr; and, as ever, the reliably conscientious staff at Conwy Library.

BIBLIOGRAPhy

GENERAL

DEACON, Richard. *Madoc and the Discovery of America*. Frederick Muller, London, 1967.

PUGH, Ellen. *Brave His Soul*. Dodd, Mead & co. New York, 1970.

STEPHENS, Thomas. *Madoc – an essay on the discovery of America by Madoc ab Owain Gwynedd.* Longmans, London, 1893.

WILLIAMS, Gwyn. *Madoc – The Making of a Myth*. Eyre Methuen, London, 1979

NORTH AMERICAN INDIANS

CATLIN, George. *North American Indians*. Penguin Books, New York, 1989.

MARRIOTT, Alice, & RACHLIN, Carol K. *American Indian Mythology*, New American Library, New York, 1972.

THE VIKING VOYAGES

KURLANSKY, Mark. *Cod – a biography of the fish that changed the world*. Jonathan Cape, London., 1998.

MORISON, Samuel E. *The European Discovery of America*, Oxford University Press, 1971.

WAHLGREEN, Eric. *The Vikings in America.*

JOHN EVANS

WILLIAMS, Prof. David. *John Evans and the Legend of Madoc 1770-1799*. University of Wales Press, 1963.

WILLIAMS, Gwyn. *John Evans's Mission to the Madogwys, 1792-1799*. Bulletin of the Board of Celtic Studies xxvii (1978).

THE OLD STONE FORTS OF TENNESSEE AND GEORGIA

BRADLEY, Jeff. *The Tennessee Handbook*. 2nd ed. Moon Publishing, Chicago CA., 1999.

FAULKNER, Charles H. *The Old Stone Fort*. University of Tennessee Press, 1968.

Other investigations by Michael Senior

£4.50

£5.50

£3.50